I Can't Believe
I Just Did That

I Can't Believe
I Just Did That

How embarrassment can wreak havoc in your life—and what you can do to conquer it

David Allyn, Ph.D.

Jeremy P. Tarcher/Penguin
a member of Penguin Group (USA) Inc.
New York

Most Tarcher/Penguin books are available at special quantity discounts for bulk purchase for sales promotions, premiums, fund-raising, and educational needs. Special books or book excerpts also can be created to fit specific needs. For details, write Penguin Group (USA) Inc. Special Markets, 375 Hudson Street, New York, NY 10014.

Jeremy P. Tarcher/Penguin
a member of
Penguin Group (USA) Inc.
375 Hudson Street
New York, NY 10014
www.penguin.com

First trade paperback edition 2004

Library of Congress Cataloging-in-Publication Data

Allyn, David (David Smith)
I can't believe I just did that : how embarrassment can wreak havoc
in your life—and what you can do to conquer it / David Allyn—1st pbk. ed.
p.   cm.
Includes bibliographical references and index.
ISBN 1-58542-361-0 (pbk.)
1. Embarrassment.   2. Embarrassment—Prevention.   3. Courage.
4. Success—Psychological aspects.   I. Title.
BF575.E53A45   2004b   2004051698
152.4—dc21

Printed in the United States of America
1   3   5   7   9   10   8   6   4   2

Book design by Barbara Sturman

contents

For Jordan

introduction The Magic of Achievement

I must have been nine years old. I'd never played softball before. For various reasons, I'd never once picked up a bat or tried on a glove. But on that day our P.E. class trekked to the makeshift school softball field. It was hot, and I felt uncomfortable in my helmet. When I got up to bat, the ball came at me, and I closed my eyes. I made a sorry attempt at a swing. When I opened my eyes again, all the kids in the outfield were laughing. Someone said something to someone else, and everyone moved in closer. I could feel the hot flush of embarrassment in my cheeks.

A voice in my head said, *How could I have done that?*

Another pitch, another swing, more laughs.

That's how it went every time we played. I grew more and more self-conscious, more and more ashamed.

Eventually I came to a decision: No more team sports.

Not only did I stop playing team sports (except at school, where we had no choice), but I also lost all interest in watching sports as a spectator. For many, many years I adamantly refused to talk about sports, until one day Jack, a colleague at Princeton University, where I was then teaching, asked me to play on the department baseball team. I immediately said no. Not a chance.

But he pressed. He knew I was interested in the science of achievement from both a scholarly and a personal point of view. At the time, in fact, I was taking a seminar on personal development as a result of which I was having breakthroughs in many areas of my life. Still, I had a personal policy: *No team sports.*

"Come on," he said. "You know you want to."

He was right, of course. I wanted, deep down, to play. I wanted the freedom to swing out and have fun. Twenty years after embarrassing myself on the softball field, I still envied anyone who felt really confident in life, confident enough to try something without worrying about looking like a fool. I knew that until I could be relaxed about failure, I would never be the kind of person I secretly dreamed of being: capable, composed, commanding. And I thought that maybe, just maybe, I could reinvent myself. Maybe I could hit the ball—hard.

When I first got near the baseball field, it was like elementary school all over again. I had a pit in my stomach. I was sure I would humiliate myself. When I got up to bat, I didn't miss the ball, but I did hit a pop fly that dropped right into the pitcher's glove.

Several games, several pop flies, and plenty of frustration later, I decided enough was enough. *How could I have been so stupid as to join a team?* Sports weren't for me. Who was I kidding? I was letting my team down, not to mention my friend Jack, so I would quit and make everyone happy.

But, God, I wanted to be able to play well. I looked at Jack. What did he know that I didn't?

I stopped him as everyone else was leaving. "Hey, Jack. What is it?" I asked. "Why can't I do this?"

"It's no big deal," he said, putting down the bag of equipment he was carrying. "You just have to shift your weight when you swing."

I had no idea what he was talking about.

"Come here, I'll show you." We walked over to the plate, and he handed me a bat. "You have to shift your weight from your back leg to your front leg. Otherwise you're making your arms do all the work."

I didn't believe that anything so simple could make a difference. But I practiced a few times, stepping forward with my left leg as I cut the air with the bat. Then Jack trotted out to the pitcher's mound. He threw me a smooth pitch and I swung. The bat connected with the ball and it went sailing, deep into right field.

"I don't believe it," I said.

He looked at me and smiled. "You're a natural."

Spirals of Shame/Spirals of Success

That moment on the field altered my life. Prior to that moment I thought there were things I just wasn't capable of. But when I hit that ball clean and hard, I knew I'd triumphed over my own beliefs about myself, about others, about life. That moment was the beginning of a spiral of success that would ultimately impact my writing, my teaching, and my relationships with others. It's not that I became a star athlete or went professional (hardly), but from that moment my perspective on life transformed. And my interactions with others transformed too.

Let's be clear: This book isn't about sports or being good at sports. It's about transforming our spirals of self-consciousness and shame into spirals of success and personal satisfaction. Chances are, there is some area of life in which you'd like to accomplish things you're not now accomplishing, be it work, school, or the dating arena. Maybe you dream of being a brilliant public speaker, or publishing your first novel, or having a truly honest and intimate relationship with someone. But you've tried in the past, you've failed, and you've decided never to try again.

For some of us, self-consciousness causes us to withdraw, to limit the risks we'll take. Instead of playing the game at hand, we wait on the sidelines, hoping for the day when we'll feel confident enough to go for it. For others, self-consciousness means perpetual worry about getting in trouble or getting kicked off the team. For others, self-consciousness means defensiveness, uncontrollable lashing out. No matter how it affects us, self-consciousness has a way of spiraling out of control—a panicky thought leads to a rash decision that leads to misunderstanding and miscommunication—spawning more withdrawal, more deception, or more defensiveness.

When we get trapped in a spiral of shame it affects the ways we communicate about money, work, sex, love, and health. Our shame spirals affect the choices we make, the ways we react and interact. And they affect the ways others react to us. All too often our shame spirals wreak havoc on our lives, our relationships, our families. Yet we rarely recognize the extent to which embarrassment and shame run our lives, the extent to which they determine our responses to everyday events, the extent to which they limit our chances of producing extraordinary results.

Fortunately, it's possible to break free from our spirals of shame. It's possible to reinvent relationships, families, careers. It's possible to break the grip of self-consciousness. And that means it's possible to turn a spiral of shame into a spiral of success. This book gives you the tools to do just that.

The Secret of Self En-Couragement

There are many embarrassing and shame-inducing situations that can be avoided. We can steer clear of embarrassment simply by keeping our promises and obeying the law. We can do ourselves a favor by eschewing gossip and focusing on the best in others. The pages that follow include numerous such suggestions for reducing the stress of "getting caught."

But sometimes self-consciousness is unavoidable. We make a mistake, we say the wrong thing, and we're mortified by what we've done. Unfortunately, how to handle difficult situations effectively is not a subject that is taught in school. At best, you and I deal with our mistakes by laughing them off; at worst, we deal with them by hiding, lying, or lashing out. But there is an alternative approach to handling embarrassing and awkward situations. This book will teach you how to develop what I call Social Courage. Having Social Courage means being able to apologize, to ask for help, to try again. Being socially courageous can make a difference in every area of your life: on line at the grocery store or on line chatting with a colleague. The greatest advantage of being socially courageous is that it allows you to transform your spirals of shame into spirals of success.

Being socially courageous can be as small as raising your hand during a meeting or asking someone special on a date. It may be asking for support from a friend or telling the truth when the truth is hard to tell. Without a doubt, it takes the courage to revisit our relationships, to examine and, if necessary, revise the ways we communicate and interact.

How do we train ourselves to be socially courageous? Through *Self En-Couragement*. Self En-Couragement is a powerful, practical approach to building the skills of social interaction. With social courage comes the freedom to break out of profitless, counterproductive beliefs and habits. Social courage makes it possible to take a new approach to social interaction, an approach that is informed and intelligent, that will serve you and serve others. Ultimately, training yourself to be courageous makes possible an ever-expanding experience of accomplishment and achievement.

Throughout this book we'll be looking at techniques for Self En-Couragement. We'll be covering simple practices to build the muscle of everyday bravery. Fortunately, we have a dozen opportunities to En-Courage ourselves each and every day: at work, at home, even at the doctor's office or at the mall. And as we get skilled at En-Couraging ourselves, we can then En-Courage others around us: our employees, our colleagues, our intimate partners, our family members, and our children. Then they too will be able to turn their spirals of self-consciousness and shame into spirals of success.

To triumph over self-consciousness, to achieve the goal of freedom in everyday life, we have to recognize how it is that we get in our own way—how we undermine our relationships, sabotage our dreams, damage our careers—*all the while thinking we're acting in our own self-interest.* We have to recognize the schemes and strategies we rely upon to avoid getting "hurt" in life, schemes and strategies that don't really work anyway and often end up hurting us. When you understand the dynamics of human interaction, you can then defeat self-consciousness and interrupt the spiral of shame so that you can live true to yourself.

In the following pages we'll be looking at the image-control tactics you and I use to avoid looking bad in life. We'll explore how we withdraw to avoid humiliation, how we make up stories to cover our tracks, how we lash out to avoid looking inward. We'll see how these image-control tactics frequently cause us to miscommunicate and make critical mistakes that cost us in our personal and professional lives. We'll also see how to replace these schemes with more effective, courageous ways of interacting, ways that are far more fulfilling and productive.

No single book has all the answers, but I hope you find this one informative, inspiring, and en-couraging. Whether you use this book to improve your relationships with your coworkers, with your family, or with your friends, I think you will find that it provides a clear path toward more satisfying interactions on a day-to-day basis. There's no reason you should have to live with self-consciousness. You deserve to know all the skills of social success. That way, the next time you say to yourself *"I Can't Believe I Just Did That!"* you can say it, not with the ache of shame but with the glowing satisfaction of pride.

PART I

Spirals of Shame

chapter 1 Image Control

You've just sent an e-mail to a friend listing your boss's worst qualities. Now you look at your screen and realize you accidentally cc'd your boss. Stunned by your own carelessness, you don't know what to do. You could offer your resignation or slip out the back door or just hide at your cubicle pretending to be busy and hope that your boss somehow misses the e-mail. One thing you know for sure, you won't be going to the office party tonight. You may, in fact, call in sick tomorrow and stay out for a week or two.

When we make mistakes, we tend to react impulsively, often unwisely. Rarely do we pause long enough to examine the situation from the other person's perspective. Rarely do we think through all of our options, weighing each carefully and with due consideration for the potential consequences of our actions.

Sometimes it's not *having made* a mistake that's the problem; it's *the fear* of making one. You want to ask someone out on a date, but you're sure you'll get snubbed. Or you want to start your own business, but you dread the idea of failing. You want to say something in a meeting, but you're worried you'll sound like you don't know what you're talking about.

One thing is clear: When we are self-conscious, we become ineffective. We easily get trapped in a spiral of shame and embarrassment. The spiral can grow and grow until it wreaks havoc on our personal or professional relationships.

But any spiral of shame can be transformed into a spiral of success. When you deal effectively with self-consciousness (i.e., with feelings of embarrassment, shame, guilt, self-resentment, and self-blame), you are better able to communicate with others, to take in and process information, to recognize your own habits of faulty thinking, and to contend with obstacles as they arise. In other words, you are able to interact more wisely and live more happily.

I have long been interested in the study of social interaction and the problem of self-consciousness. I wrote my doctoral dissertation on the sexual revolution of the 1960s and '70s, a period in which Americans were actively protesting against the shaming influences of church and state. Through the process of researching and writing that book, I discovered the extent to which the personal courage of individuals can transform society as a whole. I also saw how difficult it can be to summon and/or maintain social courage, especially in times of financial hardship.

In addition to researching and writing about social interaction, I have also had the opportunity and privilege to lead courses and training programs for both adults and young people. I have worked with many individuals eager to develop their social and leadership skills, and I have found that self-consciousness—especially as it is manifested in feelings of embarrassment, shame, and fear of looking foolish—is an issue for people from every background, every walk of life.

The more I have studied self-consciousness and the more workshops I've led the more I've come to see how easily we get trapped in spirals of shame and embarrassment. We are all stopped to some degree by our concerns about seeming:

Different * Stupid * Weak * Uncool
Unworthy * Unlikable * Unlovable * Gawky
Greedy * Stingy * Smug * Etc.

The list could go on forever.

After we do something that we think is embarrassing, we impulsively try to recover. Sometimes we try to slip away in secrecy. Other times we try to fix the mess through fabrication. And sometimes we think the best defense is a good offense, so we lash out. But all too often our recovery efforts only make things worse. Then we end up more embarrassed by our own behavior, more ashamed by the way we have (mis)handled the situation.

Truth be told, our relationships at work, at home, and everywhere in between are plagued by such spirals of self-consciousness and shame. We are constantly trying to recover from past mistakes. That makes for a lot of miscommunication and misinteraction.

I call our recovery efforts *Image Control*.[1] Our image-control tactics are what we use to avoid looking bad. Three of the most common—and the three we'll be looking at most closely in this book—are withdrawal, deception, and intimidation. Withdrawal refers to the process of pulling in or pulling back. Imagine going to a cocktail party and avoiding a colleague because you forgot to get him something for his birthday. That's withdrawal. Deception is used to hide mistakes, private secrets, personal "flaws," etc. You're late for your date. Instead of telling the truth that you waited until the last minute to leave the house, you concoct a story about the traffic. Intimidation is a strategy for keeping others at bay. For instance, your mother criticizes you during Christmas dinner. Later that evening, you can't help but point out how ridiculous it is that she saves every last scrap of aluminum foil.

Our image-control ploys aren't very sophisticated nor do they work as effectively as we would like them to.

The only way we can stop our shame spirals from intensifying is by recognizing when we're being run by self-consciousness. When we do that, we can start to catch ourselves as we try to recover through the use of image-control tactics.

We can conquer self-consciousness by training and motivating ourselves to be courageous, courageous in daily, ordinary situations. Taking risks we would rather not take (like saying hello to an attractive stranger in a museum); telling truths we would rather not tell ("I yelled at you last night because I was feeling guilty about cheating on my taxes"). Training and motivating ourselves to be courageous is the pathway to having real confidence. The more courageous we are, the more risks we take, the more confident we become.

The personal-development approach outlined in this book is called *Self En-Couragement*. Self En-Couragement is not complex or difficult. In fact, it is fairly straightforward. But it *does* take a strong commitment to your own personal growth and a willingness to take risks that may at first seem unfamiliar and uncomfortable. Fortunately, the long-term results are well worth the effort.

The more I have worked with adults and young people, the more I have become aware of the importance of building the skills of social courage. Self En-Couragement makes it possible to accomplish the seemingly un-accomplishable. I have seen people turn impending divorces into intimate, rekindled relationships. I have seen people dramatically increase their salaries, rapidly expand their companies, and realize their professional dreams. I have seen people end years of bickering and resentment in their families. I have seen students go from D's and F's to straight A's. I have quite literally seen people reinvent themselves and their lives.

Image Anxiety

I recently overheard the following conversation in a swimming pool:

Woman A:	Come on, we gotta go out tonight. It's been weeks since we've been out.
Woman B:	You can go out, but I ain't going out. Nah-uh.
Woman A:	Come on, you look fine.
Woman B:	I look like I have a bun in the oven.
Woman A:	You do have a bun in the oven.
Woman B:	Yeah, well I don't need everyone in some bar looking at me saying "Oooh, she's gonna be givin' birth any minute. Watch out. Call a doctor."
Woman A:	You're only two months pregnant. You're not even showing yet.
Woman B:	I told you, I'm not going out.

Even though I had the opportunity to observe her in a bathing suit, I would never have known that Woman B was pregnant; she looked fairly slim. But her actual appearance didn't matter to her. She was convinced that going out would be embarrassing, so she was determined to stay in.

All of us are constantly assessing ourselves, comparing ourselves to others (both real and imagined). We arrive at instantaneous conclusions: "I'm ugly." "I'm stupid." "I'm uninteresting." "I'm bad." "I'm different." These self-assessments, often based on little or no evidence, lead to self-consciousness. When we're feeling self-conscious, we rely on image-control strategies to protect ourselves. Occasionally these strategies really do serve our own best interests, but much of the time they are counterproductive. All too often you and I are like that woman in the pool. We want to go out, but we're afraid to, so we don't. That has costs. Like career-advancement opportunities. Dating opportunities. Opportunities for greater intimacy. Opportunities for educational advancement. Opportunities for personal networking. Our image-control strategies can result in self-frustration, self-resentment, and self-loathing. Not infrequently, our image-control efforts result in our feeling separate, isolated, and misunderstood. The long-term result is anomie, a deep sense of loneliness and despair.

Three of the most common—and self-defeating—image-control ploys are withdrawal, deception, and intimidation. We'll be looking closely at these three strategies in Chapters 2, 3, and 4. Each of us occasionally relies on one or more of these image-control ploys when we're feeling self-conscious. In some cases we are well aware of our image-control strategizing. In other cases, perhaps most cases, we don't recognize that we are engaged in image control. We believe we are doing what we "have" to do, or what "anyone else" would do, or what is the "only right thing" to do.

Often, we're not the least bit aware of our own image-control efforts. We do things out of self-consciousness with no idea of what we're doing. Researchers at the State University of New York at Albany observed young men buying magazines at the college bookstore. They found that those who purchased *Playboy, Penthouse,* or another men's magazine were more likely to also purchase a piece of candy or a bag of chips than those who purchased magazines like *Time* or *Newsweek.* The extra item was a face-saving device intended to legitimatize the transaction. (It's like saying, "Don't judge me. I really came in to buy other things."[2]) The guys didn't necessarily realize that's why they were buying the extra items, but their nervousness and self-consciousness ruled the day. Most of us buy "extra items" all the time: We spend emotional, psychological, and sometimes financial resources out of a concern for what others will think of us.

You might begin to reflect on the "extra items" you purchase on a daily basis to compensate for feelings of embarrassment. What steps do you take to fit in or avoid criticism? To what lengths do you go to avoid seeming difficult, demanding, or self-important? How much time and energy do you spend thinking about the things you really would do if you had the courage to do them?

Self-consciousness can limit the options we see before us. Imagine you are looking for somewhere to have lunch, and you come across a city park. It's clean and clearly safe, and there's a free bench. But the park is empty; no one else is around. Chances are you won't stay. Studies show that people are less likely to frequent city parks if those parks are empty, even if they are obviously clean and safe.[3] Being visibly alone in a public place makes us self-conscious. That doesn't mean that spending an extra few minutes to find a busy park is a bad thing, but sometimes we overlook great opportunities (for advancing our careers, for forwarding our relationships, for making a difference in the world) because we're so preoccupied with our own thoughts about what others will think of us.

Again, think about the options you overlook on a daily basis. Consider the conversations you automatically rule out. Who are the people you never talk to? What are the requests you never make? To what extent are you stopped day in and day out by your fears of looking bad?

The Origins of Image Control

You might wonder how, as a species, we became so concerned with image control. Actually, anthropologists believe that our tendencies toward image control are rooted in our evolutionary heritage. Among higher-order mammals, conflict over resources results in social ranking. Dominant individuals claim privileges over more submissive ones. In such animal societies, the more dominant individuals communicate their dominance through displays of strength (intimidation), and the more submissive individuals communicate their submissiveness through displays of weakness (appeasement). This behavior prevents conflict. Take monkeys, for example. Whenever other monkeys come close, a dominant monkey will screech to show his strength. Submissive monkeys will display signs of "surrender" by looking down, lying on the ground, and whimpering. These appeasement signals allow the submissive monkey to look weak and to help avert further power struggles.[4] They also ensure that the more dominant members of the group will share resources peacefully.

At some level, we're not very different from our primate cousins. When we want to display strength, we get loud and snappish. When we want to display harmlessness and lack of guile, we blush, we look down.

Unlike other primates, however, we rely on much more elaborate forms of image control. We have verbal ways of hiding our true thoughts, we have systems for screening our calls, we have politically savvy means for putting other people down. But to our advantage, unlike monkeys and apes, we can develop our powers of self-awareness. We can *choose* whether or not to rely on our image-control ploys. That means we can also choose to act courageously, to reject our feelings of shame and embarrassment in favor of bold interaction.

The Pros and Cons of Self-Consciousness

Self-consciousness isn't always a bad thing. It can, in fact, be a very positive force. The fear of rebuke can stop people from acting in anti-social or selfish ways. The fear of looking foolish can motivate someone to study hard before a big test or prepare thoroughly before a public presentation. A certain amount of effort expended on reputation management is vital for both personal and professional advancement. People who are indifferent to social cues rarely get ahead. People who don't pay attention to the basics of "fitting in"—dressing appropriately, playing by the company/cultural rules, being on time, keeping agreements—are likely to lose out in life.

Fortunately, you and I can't help but be self-conscious to a certain degree. Likewise, we have some biologically inherited face-saving skills that work brilliantly. Take blushing, for instance. When people blush, they become (for lack of a better word) *attractive*. If you see someone blushing, chances are you will feel compassion or empathy for that person. You certainly won't see that person as a threat or a fraud. Blushing is the body's way of saying "Please take pity on me." And it is a remarkably effective form of communication. In fact, studies show that children who blush when chastised get punished less severely than those who act defiant. Other studies show that an adult who blushes (or otherwise acts ashamed) after knocking down a grocery store display will get fewer critical looks than a person who acts indifferent.

Blushing works. So, in some cases, does showing your strength. That's because genuine confidence is compelling. In the corporate world, for instance, no one wants a self-deprecating neurotic for a company commander. You want a CEO or a CFO or a division chief who is going to be more brazen than bashful, more alpha wolf than inner child.

But there are three problems with our image-control ploys. The first is that, on average, we are *overly* self-conscious creatures. We *over*estimate the risks of being ridiculed. We *over*-worry about what people are thinking about us. So we imagine that others are reveling in our every failure, our every flaw.

Two professors conducted a study on self-consciousness. In the study, a group of students were asked to sit in a room and fill out phony surveys. Then, another student wearing a geeky Barry Manilow T-shirt would be sent into the room. In each trial, a different group of students were asked to fill out surveys, and a different student was sent in. After each trial, the T-shirt wearer was asked to estimate how many people in the room noticed what was on his shirt. In almost every case, the T-shirt wearer overestimated the number of people who'd been paying attention to his outfit.[5] This is the "imaginary spotlight" effect. When we take risks, we think we're "in the spotlight" far more than we really are.

The second problem with image control is that it all too often leads to drastic miscommunication. If you decide to keep to yourself, there's a good chance your shy countenance will be mistaken for aloofness. If you decide to act tough, who's to say your tough act won't be read as hostility? The fact is: our image-control ploys are frequently misinterpreted by others.

The third problem with image control is that we often rob ourselves of opportunities to interact in ways that would further our own interests. Consider an aspiring writer who, afraid of embarrassment, doesn't go up to an editor at a cocktail party and say hello. Or a would-be actor who can "never find the time" to go on auditions. Or a young lawyer who doesn't admit to his more senior colleagues that he's unfamiliar with the legal terms they're using. In these cases, it's obvious that self-consciousness is the culprit and that the price for trying to avoid embarrassment is high.

But you and I act out of self-consciousness all the time; we just don't always realize it. Overly cautious, we pull in, or we lash out, or we trump up the truth. Those choices tend to rob us of our effectiveness, our freedom, our ability to communicate. Imagine the following scenarios:

* Laura wants to reschedule a meeting with a client so that she can go to her son's soccer game, but, worried that she'll lose the client's respect, she doesn't even make the request. (Then, when she does go to the meeting, she can barely concentrate because all she's thinking about is her son's game.)

* Mac senses his coworkers feel that he "doesn't belong," so he keeps a low profile, remaining quiet during meetings and eating lunch alone at his desk. As a result, Mac misses out on opportunities to show he is a team player.

* Christina doesn't understand the material in class, so she never raises her hand to participate in the discussion. As a result, she never gets clarification on the material. (And the professor figures she hasn't done the reading.)

By engaging in unnecessary image control, we make a mess of things in our personal lives too:

* Allysa fears that her boyfriend is having second thoughts. Not wanting to get hurt, she starts to play it cool. But that only causes him to question the relationship more.

* Brandon assumes that his ultrasuccessful brother will think he's stupid for quitting his job, so Brandon doesn't return his phone calls. But that just makes their relationship more strained.

* Cathy tells her best friend that her short story is about the Wild West when it's really about the friend. The story gets published, and the only thing Cathy can think about is how her friend is going to react. Cathy is unable to enjoy the experience of being a published author.

Decisions like these lead to all sorts of problems in our personal relationships and our professional lives. Very quickly we end up feeling anxious, ashamed, and angry at ourselves and others.

Misreactive Moves

My first venture into the world of sales was one that I will never forget. At ten years old I began selling Christmas cards. The more cards I sold, the more points I got. The points could be used to buy anything from a set of encyclopedias to a telescope. I wanted the telescope, and I needed two hundred points to get it. Fearlessly I went from door to door urging people to select designs from the Christmas card catalogue. I was very successful and got scores of orders.

Two months later, the company sent me boxes and boxes of cards to deliver to my customers. But I'd forgotten to write down which customers had ordered which designs. I had no idea how to distribute the boxes of cards correctly.

I was so embarrassed by my own neglectfulness that I never distributed the cards at all. Instead I dumped all the boxes in the trash and tried to forget about them. The customers had paid for their cards, but they never received them. They were taken away with the day's garbage.

I did get my telescope, but I couldn't even look at it. It stayed in my closet, unopened. I continued to be embarrassed, so I avoided the neighbors as much as I could. When I had to walk through the neighborhood, I would do everything necessary to avoid running into a former customer. In the moment in which fear of embarrassment strikes, it almost always seems like there is some other, *real* danger present: the possibility of getting in trouble, getting hurt, getting rejected, getting fired. We are practically incapable of seeing out own anxieties about embarrassment. (In fact, we don't want to see them, because having anxiety about embarrassment is, for most of us, fairly embarrassing.) So, instead of taking a rational approach to potentially embarrassing situations—an approach in which we calmly weigh the pros and cons of action—we say to ourselves, "No way, I couldn't do that!"

My decision to toss the unopened boxes of Christmas cards into the trash was the rash decision of a child, but, more important, it was an example of an impulsive image-control ploy. I didn't think through the consequences of throwing out the boxes; I was completely focused on avoiding the immediate danger of loss of face. In retrospect, it is also clear my decision was misreactive. It created more problems than it solved. It is obvious I should have explained my mistake to my customers or, at the very least, asked someone else for advice. But at the time I panicked. And, of course, my impulsive misreaction created a far bigger mess—for my customers, for my parents, and for me—than my original mistake of not writing down who ordered what.

I can only imagine what the neighbors must have thought: "What an obnoxious, thieving kid!" Probably some of them decided they would never give money to a kid who came to their door selling something again. In other words, my misreaction may very well have increased the overall level of dissociality in the neighborhood for years to come.

That's what image-control ploys do. They breed animosity, distrust, and/or anxiety. Hence the importance of understanding our image-control ploys and their often misreactive nature, because children aren't the only ones who make rash decisions or who fail to think through all the consequences of a possible decision or who fail to get input from other sources before acting. We adults make impulsive mis-interactional moves all the time.

The Psychic Costs of Image Control

Impulsive image control has opportunity costs and can lead to misunderstandings and misinteractions. But that's not all. Image control is stressful. It affects personal well-being. It negatively impacts the body, the mind, and the spirit.

Studies show that when we try to manage the impression that others have of us, our stress levels go up. Over time image control can lead to acne, aging, high blood pressure, even hair loss. Those symptoms usually provoke additional anxiety, which leads to social withdrawal and further efforts at image control, and, in turn, more stress. It's a vicious cycle. We withdraw, lie, or lash out; we get stressed; our bodies show signs of wear; we strategize more.

The stress caused by image control has a negative effect on mental acuity. People who suppress their emotions are more distracted, remember less, and process information less accurately. This can lead to misassessments, miscommunication, and bad decision making. From a cognitive-skills perspective, image control is highly disadvantageous.[6]

As image control takes a toll on the body and the mind, it also takes a toll on the spirit. While social scientists haven't done as much empirical research on the psychic costs of image control, the evidence is becoming increasingly clear. When one pulls in, makes up stories, or lashes out, one becomes less engaged with others; more concerned with embarrassment, failure, and humiliation; and less enthusiastic about job opportunities, family activities, even social activities. Overall one becomes less excited about life. As we take a cautious or hostile approach to interacting with others, our regrets and resentments accumulate, ultimately leading to a state of self-disrespect or even disgust.[7]

Embarrassment Versus Shame

It is important to address the often misunderstood distinction between embarrassment and shame. Embarrassment results from a perceived collapse of *social* image. We get embarrassed when we think others are viewing us in a negative light. Embarrassment usually results from sudden exposure (i.e., a swimsuit coming off in the water), loss of bodily control (getting one's period at the wrong moment), avoidable gaffes (spelling mistakes in a business letter), sudden blemishes (a bright red pimple), and/or dismissal (getting laughed at by better-dressed strangers in a dance club). Shame, on the other hand, results from a collapse of *self*-image. We feel shame when we view ourselves in a negative light. Shame typically follows from the conclusion that we have violated our own principles or failed to live up to our own standards of conduct.

But shame and embarrassment are not so easily disentangled. For the most part we arrive at our self-image through the early internalization of opinions, viewpoints, and beliefs of significant *others*. Thus self-image is actually formulated in a *social* context, so the experience of shame is almost always also the experience of embarrassment. If you can, think back to when you were a child. You did something and got yelled at for it. You concluded you were "bad." Now, any time you are "bad" you feel a mixture of shame and embarrassment. It's not just shame or just embarrassment; it's both.

For our purposes, what is most important is that the experience of minor embarrassment can quickly lead to image-control efforts that result in feelings of deep shame: for instance, if you call someone by the wrong name and then impulsively make up a lie to explain your gaffe. Because lying almost always leads to self-disrespect—no matter how small the lie—the end result is a certain degree of shame. This shame will often lead to another shame-causing move (e.g., you say something mean-spirited to a third party about the person you've lied to in an unconscious attempt to discredit that person), which leads to a response (the person finds out you've been talking negatively about him/her and confronts you about it), yet another shame-causing move (e.g., you lie yet again), another response (the person files a formal complaint about you), and so on, until the spiral of shame has grown out of control.

The opposite of a shame spiral is a success spiral. In a success spiral, success leads to pride, which leads to more confidence, which leads to more success, which leads to more pride, etc., etc. Success does not mean success only in the career realm (though it does include this); it also means the achievement of healthy, satisfying relationships; the achievement of personal goals; and the achievement of deep fulfillment. In other words, it means success in every area of life.

Social Shame

On a social level, shame and embarrassment are important. As Colin Powell has written, echoing the sentiments of many: "We seem to have lost our sense of shame as a society. Nothing seems to embarrass us; nothing shocks us anymore. Spend time switching channels on daytime television and you will find a parade of talk shows serving up dysfunctional people whose morally vacant behavior offers the worst possible models for others."

I couldn't agree more with this assessment. But I would argue that what looks like "shameless" behavior is often behavior that is driven by shame. The aggressive, almost violent use of four-letter words; the active rebellion against social norms; the refusal to acknowledge the needs of others, especially those of children—these are crude forms of lashing out. They represent collective shame in its rawest form. This is the shame of having lied, cheated, and exploited others. It's the shame of having given up on dreams. It's the shame of having let down parents, teachers, and mentors. It's the shame of having been arrogant, willfully ignorant, and cowardly. We need to be training young people to recognize their image-control strategies so that they can break free from their spirals of shame and engage in behavior that will lead to real and lasting success. We certainly don't want young people to mature into leaders who would lie to defend their actions or perpetuate wars to avoid the embarrassment of admitting defeat.

Those of us who tolerate antisocial behavior usually do so because we are concerned about the possibility of losing face if we speak up. When we don't speak up, when we don't say no, when we don't demand change, we are just as guilty of being cowardly as those we object to. Keeping quiet is an image-control strategy. It's a way of avoiding the spotlight, a way of avoiding accountability.

It takes courage to be a good citizen, And it takes courage to demand that others be good citizens. There is always a social risk involved in pointing out bad behavior. It is much easier to turn a blind eye. Fortunately, the art and science of Self En-Couragement allows you both to build your own skills of social courage and to encourage others to build theirs.

Self-Consciousness: A Brief Survey of Recent Thought

It has taken the sciences a relatively long time to devote serious attention to exploring the role of shame and embarrassment in everyday life, though some early pioneers made important contributions to our understanding. This brief survey isn't meant to be exhaustive; it's just intended to give a flavor of the research that's already been done on self-consciousness and image control.

Freud, for one, emphasized the impact of childhood shame on personality development, connecting shame to the emergence of the superego.[8] For Freud, childhood shame was connected to unconscious, incestuous desires—erotic longing for the parent of the other sex. The neo-Freudians, though they shifted focus from the unconscious to the conscious, recognized the importance of shame in the creation of character. They saw a link between early experiences of humiliation and the development of a defensive, repressive personality. Neo-Freudians like Alfred Adler and Erik Erikson encouraged parents to take a nurturing rather than chastising approach to child rearing. Adler warned that early feelings of shame could lead to a lifelong "inferiority complex" or, perhaps even worse, "a drive for power."

The study of face-saving and impression management was significantly advanced by the mid-century sociologist Erving Goffman, who pioneered the study of pretense. Using the language of theater, he showed how we "play roles" in daily life: how we behave one way with our coworkers and another with our friends, for instance. Like Freud before him, Goffman illuminated how much we hide our true thoughts and feelings on a day-to-day, moment-by-moment basis. (His work has now been further developed by Judith Butler, a scholar who focuses on gender, sexuality, and "the performance of everyday life," and James C.

Scott, who distinguishes between our "public transcripts"—what we say aloud—and our "private transcripts"—what we keep to ourselves.)

Shame and its negative impact on the realization of one's full potential were crucial themes in the work of Abraham Maslow, Albert Ellis, and other human-potential-movement psychologists of the fifties and sixties. Self-consciousness was also an implicit theme in the groundbreaking work of the transactional analysts of the sixties and seventies, like best-selling writers Eric Berne and Thomas Harris, who examined commonplace yet counterproductive patterns of behavior. The transactional analysts demonstrated how shame and embarrassment can lead to game-playing, which often leads to bitterness, resentment, and regret. Researchers in the 1970s also began important work exploring the biological and developmental sources of shyness, embarrassment, shame, aggression, and self-consciousness.

It wasn't until the 1980s, however, that social scientists began paying significant attention to the potentially dangerous impact of shame and embarrassment on social life. As concerns grew about eating disorders and the spread of sexually transmitted diseases like AIDS, the problem of shame entered the spotlight. When health educators tried to encourage open discussion about these issues, they became aware of the powerful effects of self-consciousness on communication and personal decision making.

In the wake of the feminist and gay-liberation movements, much has been written on the negative effects of sexual shame and bodily shame. Meanwhile, society has benefited from several decades of humanistic advancement. Practices that were once common in schools—corporal punishment, the use of scare tactics in "family-life" classes, the use of sexist and heterosexist epithets by teachers—are now increasingly being regarded as unacceptable.

Still, the study of shame and embarrassment is just in its infancy, in part because scholars are often ashamed or embarrassed to study these aspects of emotional life. Francis Broucek, the author of a psychoanalytic treatise on shame, recalls, "When friends and acquaintances learned that

I was writing a book, they would invariably ask about the subject of the book; when I replied that I was writing about shame, a frequent response was 'Oh,' followed either by an awkward silence or a prompt change of subject. . . . Shame is so painful that we hope it ends quickly; we have no particular desire to reflect on it or talk about it, because to do so runs the risk of re-experiencing it. . . . We tend to be ashamed of being ashamed and try to deny and hide our shame for that reason."[9]

Meanwhile, most of us are poorly equipped to discuss the nuances of social interaction. While we have all become familiar with the highly sophisticated vocabulary of psychology (think of terms like "libido," "sublimation," and "passive aggression") and the equally sophisticated vocabulary of sociology (consider expressions like "popular culture," "groupthink," and "generational revolt"), we are still uncomfortable when it comes to discussing everyday interaction. Everyday interaction occurs in *dyadic* (one-on-one) encounters and *network* (small-group) situations. We are simply not accustomed to thinking of ourselves as mere *interactors* reacting and responding to others. We much prefer to think of ourselves as either all-important individuals with dramatic inner lives (the psychological point of view) or as helpless victims of large-scale social forces (the sociological point of view). But if we are going to develop a systematic approach to effective interaction we are going to need to begin to regard ourselves first and foremost as interactors operating in predictable, often demonstrably ineffective, ways.

Far more so than academic scholars, creative writers and performing artists have long made social interaction the focus of their work. Fiction writers, dramatists, actors, and directors are especially skilled at portraying human interaction and misinteraction. After all, there is no such thing as a good plot without misunderstandings between characters. We can learn a great deal by paying attention to the literary and performing arts: fiction, theater, television, film, etc. Art offers a perspective on ourselves that is often more astute than the one afforded by social science.

Fortunately, social scientists are coming to realize that miscommunication and misinteraction stemming from shame and self-consciousness are critical problems in human life. In addition, there is a new and exciting focus among research psychologists on the psychology of accomplishment and fulfillment. We are witnessing a renewed interest in the science of success, an intellectual renaissance that is long past due.

In recent years the nation has undergone a dramatic and re-markable development. Throughout the country, many hundreds of thousands of people have begun working on, and improving, their in-teractional skills by participating in transformational programs, by hir-ing "life coaches," and by reading books like this one. Concepts and questions that would once have been dismissed as "soft," "touchy-feely," or "New Agey" are now being discussed and addressed by the most powerful men and women in our society. Even as the nation struggles with major issues and long-term problems, CEOs, organiza-tional leaders, and politicians (both liberal and conservative) are ac-tively inquiring into their own interactive strengths and weaknesses. We are on the verge of a major transformation in the way we under-stand and relate to our interactive practices. In fact, we may soon see a "bio-technological" revolution: a revolution in the way we apply sci-entific concepts to the living of daily life.

From Spirals of Shame to Spirals of Success: Reconstructing Our Relationships

Image control often leads to a spiraling pattern of self-resentment, miscommunication, and misinteraction. But when we interact in more effective, courageous ways, we can transform our spirals of self-consciousness and shame into spirals of achievement and success.

Rarely do we realize how important it is to train ourselves to be courageous. We think of courage as something inborn or given to us by others. But you and I have the capacity to develop our skills of social courage, and the more we do, the better able we are to catch our spirals of shame and transform them instantaneously into spirals of success.

This book is divided in two parts. In the remainder of Part I, we will concentrate on the three major strategies of image control: withdrawal, intimidation, and lying. In Part II, we'll focus on ways to break free from our spirals of shame through the art and science of Self En-Couragement. We will look closely at how Self En-Couragement can make a difference at work, with our family members, and in our most intimate relationships. Throughout the book you will find practical suggestions for implementing a constructive, self-encouraging approach to deal with difficult situations. Some of these suggestions show you how to avoid situations that will likely make you self-conscious, some show you how to deal with awkward situations once they have already occurred, and some show you how to maximize your sense of self-confidence in the face of any and all circumstances.

This book isn't meant to be read passively; it's meant to be used, studied, and grappled with. To get the most out of this book you will have to engage in self-exploration and try the techniques included throughout. You may want to purchase a notebook to record your observations about your relationships and your ways of interacting. You may want to keep track of what works for you and what doesn't. I would also recommend sharing this book with others, so that you are able to develop a community of friends, family members, and associates committed to mastering the skills of courageous interaction. If you are a teacher, I recommend sharing it with your students. If you are a manager, I recommend sharing it with your team.

You and I are about to embark on a journey. It's a journey of self-exploration and societal examination. Every journey has its challenges. The bigger the challenges, the bigger the rewards. I hope you will use this book to revitalize your relationships and reenergize your career. Every courageous action you take gives others permission to be courageous themselves.

chapter 2 The Perils of Pulling In

When Newland Archer opened the door at the back of the club box the
curtain had just gone up on the garden scene. There was no reason why
the young man should not have come earlier, for he had dined at seven,
alone with his mother and sister, and had lingered afterward over a cigar
in the Gothic library. . . . But . . . it was "not the thing" to arrive early at
the opera; and what was or was not "the thing" played a part as important
in Newland Archer's New York as the inscrutable totem terrors that had
ruled the destinies of his forefathers thousands of years ago.

— EDITH WHARTON, *THE AGE OF INNOCENCE*

Nokowanda was a very bright and talented
tenth-grade girl. Her parents had fled from Africa to the United States
and had managed, with the help of various organizations, to enroll her
in one of the finest prep schools in the country. Even in competition
with students from upper-class homes, Nokowanda excelled. Her first
semester at boarding school she got three A's and a B.

But Nokowanda had few friends. She was so shy, people found it hard to hear her when she spoke. Not only did she feel lonely most of the time, but she also had few dreams. No matter how well she did in school, most of the time she was sad.

I first met Nokowanda when she was applying to be a student in a summer leadership course I had been hired by a nonprofit organization to give to exceptionally bright minority students. When she came in for her interview, I was surprised that she was an Andover student. Andover students have a reputation for being sophisticated, extroverted go-getters. But Nokowanda practically disappeared into the pillows of the couch. I had to lean forward to hear her answers to my questions. It wasn't hard to tell that Nokowanda was afraid: afraid of being judged, afraid of saying the wrong thing, afraid of making a mistake.

Nokowanda had a strategy: stay quiet, stay small, stay as invisible as possible. It was a strategy that probably worked for her in certain contexts or had worked for her at some point in the distant past. But it nearly ruined her chances of being admitted to the program for which she was applying. I have no doubt that most interviewers would have readily dismissed her as a viable candidate. Four months later, when Nokawanda was a student in my class, I would learn that she was embarrassed by her accent and foreign-sounding name. That's why she chose shyness as an image control tactic.

In coming to her interview, Nokowanda misinteracted. She failed to take in all the pertinent information and develop an appropriate interactional style. She relied on a crude form of image control: reticence. It nearly cost her the opportunity to participate in a program she herself was eager to participate in.

We all make interactional mistakes like this day in and day out. We rely on a crude image-control ploy and then fail to get what we want. In hindsight, we blame our own "personalities," as if they were immutable and fixed in stone. We fail to realize the extent to which our interactional failures are a direct result of the strategies we employ.

Inaction

The most obvious and essential element of effective interaction is *interaction*. Nonetheless, we often do not interact at all, or we interact as little as possible, forcing others to interpolate our actual thoughts and feelings, i.e., to read between the lines of what we say and what we do. We are especially prone to noninteraction or suppressed interaction after an embarrassing or shame-inducing incident. In such cases, we are very likely to pull in, much as a turtle pulls into the protective covering of its shell. This pulling in may be obvious (like refusing to leave your home) or it may be more subtle, involving, perhaps, only the suppression of the emotions behind a façade of calm self-assurance. Regardless of the form it takes, withdrawal makes open communication and effective interaction that much more difficult.

When you do something that is embarrassing or shame-inducing, the natural inclination is to hide your face. Researchers studying tapes of the TV show *Candid Camera* have concluded that hiding one's face postembarrassment is a virtually universal response.[1] It's an automatic response to shame. When little children feel ashamed, they will physically hide behind a couch or a door. Adults don't usually have the option of hiding in such a literal fashion, so we find other ways of hiding when we feel embarrassed. We hide in a social rather than a physical sense. But hiding usually means we end up avoiding just those interactions we ought to have most.

In this chapter we will be examining a variety of different types of withdrawal strategies: from stage flight to bench-warming to emotional concealment. None of these strategies is inherently ineffective, but each has a tendency to create more problems than it solves. Because withdrawal strategies reduce communication, they usually cause confusion, misunderstanding, and misinteraction.

Stage Flight

Everyone is familiar with the concept of stage fright, but most of us don't realize how often we practice stage *flight*. "Stage flight" means actively fleeing from opportunities to speak in public. We flee at school, at work, in all sorts of situations. We don't usually know *what* it is we're fleeing from exactly, other than the burden of having to perform before a crowd.

Stage flight is an image-control tactic. Feeling self-conscious, we respond by fleeing from (seemingly) risky situations. It could be called "proactive shyness."[2]

There are good reasons for not volunteering to give public presentations, for not participating in public forums. People who speak up in public are more likely to get criticized, ridiculed, and/or shot down than people who stay quiet. Just look at history. Leaders throughout time have been attacked, mocked, even killed. Socrates was first laughed at, then arrested, then forced to choose between recanting his views or taking poison.

But anyone who turns down public-speaking opportunities, who avoids participating in meetings, who shies away from open communication is going to miss opportunities for personal advancement and achievement. Those missed opportunities are going to lead to frustration and, most likely, regret. They are going to lead to a deeper sense of shame: *why am I such a coward about public speaking?* (Besides, when was the last time you really had to worry about being forced to take poison for airing your views?)

Most of us start fleeing from public speaking at an early age. We have a particularly embarrassing or shame-inducing moment (typically at school) and subsequently avoid public speaking to every extent possible.

"One of my defining moments came in the third grade," writes Oprah Winfrey, "the day a book report I'd turned in earned my teacher's praise and made my classmates whisper, 'she thinks she's so smart.' For too many years after that, my biggest fear was that others would see me as arrogant. In some ways, even the extra weight I carried around was my apology to the world—my way of saying 'See, I really don't think I'm better than you.' The last thing I wanted was for my actions to make me appear conceited. Full of myself."[3]

Sometimes our embarrassing moments happen later in life. When Barbra Streisand was singing at a public concert in Central Park, she forgot the words to a song. After that, she didn't sing in public for another twenty-seven years.

Whether one can remember one's early embarrassments or not, the facts are clear: For most adults, "public" speaking seems dangerous or, at the very least, frightening. The risk involved is not necessarily a function of the number of people "in the audience." Some people are perfectly comfortable speaking to an audience of thousands but will try to avoid having to speak before a group of ten or twelve. And it doesn't necessarily matter *who* is in the audience. Some people are most afraid of speaking before those they highly respect; others are most afraid of speaking before their peers.

There are many ways to practice stage flight. The most obvious, of course, is to turn down a formal invitation to speak in public. But there are many more subtle ways of fleeing from "the stage." Perhaps Steve practices stage flight by keeping a low profile during business meetings. He sits where he is least likely to be noticed; maybe he even angles himself behind another colleague. Instead of volunteering his thoughts and opinions, he does his best not to get called on. He avoids eye contact with the person running the meeting. Of course, he has to disguise his flight. So he nods to show he's listening. He occasionally leans forward and then leans back. He rubs his chin. He knits his brow for a moment to imply that he's giving serious thought to what's being said, and then he nods again to show that he concurs with the speaker.

Another way of making sure you are never "onstage" is to avoid unpredictable gatherings. You get invited to a party, but you don't know who's going to be there (or what they're going to want to talk about), so you decline the invitation. Unpredictable gatherings arouse some of our greatest anxieties, perhaps because we all made blunders at parties when we were kids. Most people actively flee from unpredictable gatherings as best they can.

Another way of fleeing from social interaction is to not return phone calls and/or e-mail. It seems the more ways we find of communicating, the more tempting it is to avoid communication. Sometimes embarrassment or shame sends us turning off our cell phones, canceling our phone service, changing our e-mail addresses. A human resource professional informs me that a growing problem in corporate America is managers—eager to avoid uncomfortable face-to-face conversations—firing employees by e-mail. Just imagine what it would be like to find out you've been terminated through e-mail. On the other hand, imagine how afraid of direct communication some managers are that they would deliver that news in such an impersonal way.

Most of us are ashamed of being self-conscious, so we conceal our flight patterns. We make up elaborate excuses to justify our withdrawal: "I can't go to Florida to give the talk because I have so much work to do on project X." "I didn't say anything during the meeting because I thought Jack really hit the nail on the head." "I'd love to go to the party, but I'm swamped with schoolwork." Often we try to convince ourselves too: "It's much better for the company if a vice president gives the speech than if I do it." "I *would* talk during meetings, but the meetings never lead to any real change anyway." "I *would* go to the party, but I *am* swamped with schoolwork." Not infrequently, we end up believing our own spin.

Stage flight can be highly irritating to others. Best-selling author Edmund Morris says he does his best not to have to work with people who withdraw. "I find that the more shy someone acts, the harder *I* have to work. I have to work harder to get them to express their thoughts, and I end up having to make the phone calls they are unwilling to make." However you choose to flee, the net result is usually the same. You end up feeling disappointed in yourself, you end up missing out on key opportunities, and you run the risk of damaging your relationships with others.

Quitting and Sitting on the Bench

Human beings don't like to lose. We experience failure as embarrassing, humiliating, and shameful. So we tend to play only those games at which we think we have a fairly good shot of winning. Once we fail at something, we tend to stop competing entirely. We quit. We sit out the rest of the game. If we're in a good mood, we stay on the sidelines and watch others compete.

Alyssa is a photographer who has put off compiling a portfolio of her work for ten long years, lest the portfolio turn out not to be good enough. She has dealt with her fear of rejection by adopting a strategy combining passivity and invisibility. For ten years, she has taken pictures, developed them, and thought about putting them in a portfolio that she could show to magazine editors and would-be employers. But she's never done it. Of course, the longer she holds out, the harder it will be for her to advance her career as a photographer and, ultimately, the harder it will be for her to actually avoid rejection.

Quitting and *bench warming* are ways of making sure you never lose. The only problem is, they also radically reduce the chances of success.

Unfortunately, you and I are very good at convincing ourselves that the chances of losing are higher than they really are. We'll also try to convince ourselves that the rewards of winning would be minor. So we end up quitting in careers and relationships that we would really like to stay in. We end up instead on professional tracks and in family scenarios that are safe but ultimately unsatisfying.

Gwen has dreamed for years of writing a children's book. She's even composed a few sample illustrations. But she has dozens of reasons why she hasn't written the book yet and why now "just isn't a good time." Some of those reasons sound fairly logical. She is a college professor, and though teaching literature no longer excites her, she wants to get tenure before she starts doing something "silly" like writing children's books. Still, essentially, she's sitting out her career as a children's book author.

Of course, the longer you sit something out, the harder it gets to rejoin the game. At some point, it's natural to give up all hope of ever stepping back onto the field. You're then left with a sense of regret that can easily turn into self-loathing. You stay out of the game, you get mad at yourself for staying out, perhaps you make an effort to get back in, but you fail because you're now "rusty," so you get mad at yourself for failing, you stay out of the game even longer, you get mad at yourself for staying out, etc., etc., etc. Pretty soon, you're trapped in a spiral of shame.

Quitting and bench warming aren't just problems for adults. Children and teens are likely to pull out of the game after the slightest embarrassment too. That's one of the reasons it is so hard for teachers to "raise standards"; they know how quickly students will give up on themselves and their academic careers if they're criticized. And bench warming is even a problem for older people. I've met people in their nineties who are waiting for the "right time" to take a risk, wholly oblivious to the fact that the right time may not come before it's too late.

George Soros, one of the richest, most charitable, most progressive, and most admired men in the world, dreams of being a respected philosopher. Over the years he has picked up and put down his pen. At times he's thought about quitting the philosophy game; other times he's sat on the bench reading the works of others. His intellectual efforts haven't been nearly as successful as his financial and philanthropic efforts; at times, he's been ridiculed. But even if George Soros never succeeds as an intellectual, he has nothing to lose by trying, except perhaps the esteem of people who haven't accomplished nearly as much as he has.[4]

Shying Away from Setting Goals

Bench warming is one way of avoiding failure. But sometimes bench warming is impossible or impractical. A lawyer doesn't just decide to withdraw from the profession after losing a case. So how else do people avoid failure? By not "calling the shot," by shying away from setting goals. Effectively, we get *goal shy*.

The most powerful goals a person can create meet three criteria: (1) They set the bar high but not unrealistically so; (2) they contain a deadline; (3) they are announced publicly. Consider the goals set by professional athletes. Athletes set goals for themselves that require them to train hard and give their all, but they give themselves a deadline for achieving those goals, and they always declare their goals to others (coaches, trainers, friends, the press, etc.).

Those of us who aren't professional athletes are rarely so rigorous in our goal setting. We may set the bar high, but never tell anyone else. Or tell lots of people, knowing perfectly well that our goals are "pie in the sky." Or we set goals that are too low, so that there's no doubt about accomplishing them.

David is an entrepreneur whose dream is to start a chain of fast-food restaurants that will be as successful as McDonald's. But David has had several business failures in the past, so he is reluctant to share his dream with his family members, lest he make a fool of himself again.

Failing is embarrassing. That's why we don't set clear, concrete goals. We set goals that make it easy to avoid shame. When I was working for a nonprofit organization, I attended a meeting by a coalition of groups committed to providing health insurance for low-income families. At the end of the meeting I asked how many families the group intended to get insured by the end of the year. There was a hushed whisper in the room. "Well," the chairperson said, "we intend to get as many families insured as possible. At this point, we're not prepared to say anything more specific than that." They weren't willing to set a clear goal. I left the meeting doubtful about their chances of making a real difference for low-income families.[5]

Sometimes goals *can* get in the way by making us more self-conscious than we need to be. So it may help to set negative goals. An aspiring actor who has never been in a movie might aim to lose the Oscar. A person whose goal is to make a million dollars might strive to lose ten million. I recently took my daughter ice skating for the very first time. I asked her to promise that she would fall at least three times. She readily agreed. When we got on the ice she immediately fell and started crying, "Daddy, I don't like it. Take me home!" "Sweetheart," I said, "you promised you would fall at least three times." Begrudgingly she kept skating till she had fallen twice more. But by that point she'd forgotten her fears and wanted to keep skating. Falling had become part of the game. A half hour later she was skating around the rink without even holding my hand.

With my daughter, I was the one calling the shot. But when we don't have our parents (or teachers or bosses) around to do the job, that task falls upon us. We are the ones who must decide what we're going to aim for and who we're going to tell in advance.

Part of goal setting is setting your values: "My goal is to be CEO without ever lying." "My goal is to sell my invention for a million dollars without selling it to a company that pollutes the environment." "My goal is to raise a straight-A child without ever using food as a reward." We're often embarrassed to admit to ourselves that we don't know what our values are. Or we're too embarrassed to admit we're even interested in having values. Or we're afraid of the embarrassment of failing to live up to our values. So we don't think through our values carefully. We just live life haphazardly. We make decisions ad hoc without an ethical foundation to stand on. Then we end up successful but ashamed. Or unsuccessful but without any principles to take pride in.

Whether we set goals or not, we all have games we want to win. It's part of being human. Aiming blindly is still a form of aiming, it just reduces the chances of winning and increases the chances of someone else getting hit by mistake.[6]

Ineffective goal setting doesn't happen by accident. It's an image-control tactic designed to avoid the humiliation of failure. Effective goal setting doesn't happen by accident either; it takes conscious effort. But the rewards are well worth the trouble. Think of Washington, whose goal was independence from Great Britain. Or Lincoln, whose goal was holding together the Union. When you know what you're going after and you have fans rooting for you, and you know what you're willing to do and what you're not, how could you do anything but succeed?

Emotional Concealment

Mrs. G is a woman I would call an expert in the art of emotional concealment: She is always smiling, always has perfect manners, is always covered in thick layers of makeup, and always sounds as if her only interest is in helping others ("Please, let me do the dishes. . . . No, you must!"). All of this despite the fact that one of her children is a known drug dealer, the other one has all sorts of problems at school, her husband feels like a failure in his career, and Mrs. G herself has plenty of acquaintances but no close friends to turn to. Not coincidentally, Mrs. G looks twice her age, with deep wrinkles etched into her face and dark circles under her eyes. She has an aura of absolute exhaustion. The only way she might conceal her emotions more effectively would be by injecting herself with Botox.

Emotional concealment is a strategy we all practice on occasion. We feign boredom when we're excited or excitement when we're really bored. We do our best to "play it cool." We hide our sadness or conceal our anxiety. We pretend to be indifferent when we're desperately in love.

Granted there are times when emotional concealment is not only wise but also appropriate. It wouldn't make much sense to walk into a high-powered business negotiation and start weeping. It would be weird to say to someone you've just met "I hate the way you dress." But when it's overdone, emotional concealment creates a mess. It can turn dating into a power struggle, can preclude any possibility of real intimacy in our close relationships, and can put coworkers on edge. When you conceal your emotions, it encourages others to do the same. That makes every interaction a game of back-and-forth (mis)interpretation.

From an evolutionary perspective, emotional concealment apparently developed as a strategy for one primate to keep others from challenging his or her status. If a primate shows fear or happiness or anger or guilt, his status is more likely to be tested. By showing no emotions at all, he can maintain relative stability. After a male chimpanzee is defeated in a contest with another male over the rights to a female, for example, the loser will often occupy himself with a seemingly irrational activity, like intently studying his fingernails. The activity serves to hide his resentment so that he doesn't have to defend himself further. It enables him to pretend to be unconcerned with his failure.[7]

Although emotional concealment probably developed through natural selection, as humans we also have the ability to willfully hide what we're feeling. We know how to pretend we're happy when we're sad; we know how to pretend we're "fine" when we're seething with rage. Emotional masks may work for a period of time, but they become suffocating. You can pretend you're happy for a while, but the sadness will find a way out. You can pretend you're "fine" for years at a time, but the rage will find expression through passive aggression. Freud called it "the return of the repressed." What we try to deny asserts itself, sometimes in a form far more powerful and nefarious.

That doesn't mean the only answer to repression is full "liberation of the libido." There is a time and place for everything. But it does mean that we need to make more conscious and informed decisions. It's when we conceal our emotions unthinkingly—or without due consideration for the implications of our image-control efforts—that we end up in the biggest trouble.

But we rashly hide our feelings because we're worried about being judged. Instead of beaming with pride when we accomplish something great or crying when we fail, we act like it's "no big deal" so that no one thinks we care too much. Instead of saying, "I hate you right now" when our friends show up twenty minutes late, we try to keep calm and pretend nothing's wrong. (At best we might try to have a rational conversation about the importance of being on time.) This would be fine if the result weren't so often seething resentment and a profound lack of intimacy.

The effort involved in emotional concealment actually makes it harder to be rational, to think clearly, to argue logically. In fact, studies show, people who do not waste energy on emotional concealment are better able to process and remember information and to think critically about the information they have taken in. That alone is a major argument against the practice of emotional concealment in dating, in relationships, at work and at school.

Emotional concealment strategies almost inevitably lead to ever-growing spirals of shame. The less open you are, the greater the chance of miscommunication. For instance, Mark wants a promotion but acts likes he doesn't. His boss misreads his pretense of dispassion. Someone else gets promoted, and Mark ends up bitter and resentful.

We'll be discussing emotional hiding in more detail in Chapter 4 because it is not just a form of withdrawal, it is also a type of deception. We'll look at how we try to deceive others into thinking we're more excited than we are (or more blasé), more friendly (or more indifferent), more guilt ridden (or more innocent), more confident (or more insecure).

Whatever form of emotional hiding we engage in, the results are almost always the same: loss of self-esteem, loss of intimacy with others, and loss of interactional effectiveness.

Circumlocution

One way that people attempt to avoid embarrassment is by speaking "around" the point. The more direct we are, the greater the chance of what we have to say being questioned, challenged or refuted. So people speak in vague or imprecise terms. I call this circumnavigating or roundabouting. Whether people roundabout consciously or unconsciously is irrelevant. What's important to recognize is that it prevents intimacy in personal relationships and effectiveness in professional ones.

Direct statements and questions always raise the spectre of social awkwardness. If a woman asks a man, "Do you love me?" he could potentially respond a dozen different ways. "Of course I love you. What a silly question." Or "Is this about getting married again?" Or "You know I love you. That's why I bought you flowers last week." Or the kicker, "Well, I love you, but I'm not *in love* with you." So, often enough, we don't ask each other direct questions. We roundabout. "Do you want to come to my family's for Thanksgiving?" (Subtext: Do you love me?)

Just this morning the light blew out in my home office. I looked out the window and saw the super. Silly as it was, I was momentarily embarrassed to be asking for assistance with changing a lightbulb. ("How many thirty-three-year-olds with Ph.D.'s does it take to change a lightbulb?") There was no reason to be ashamed, however: I rent my apartment, the lightbulb is too high to reach without a ladder, I'm not allowed to store large items (like ladders) in the basement, etc. But those reasons weren't enough to overcome my momentary embarrassment. So when I called out the window, I phrased my request in roundabout terms. Instead of saying, "Hi, Jimmy. The lightbulb in my office is out. When could you come by and replace it?" I said, "Hi, Jimmy. The lightbulb in my office is out. It's, like, too high to replace, so I need a ladder or something." Believe it or not, I was actually surprised when I went downstairs and found a ladder waiting for me in the building foyer.

I'd assumed Jimmy would read between the lines of my request. (Of course, I used the ladder and replaced the bulb myself, so it was no big deal. But next time, when I ask him to fix the crack in the bathroom ceiling, I'm going to be certain to be more clear in my speaking.)

Students will intentionally obfuscate their prose to hide the fact that they don't know what to say (or haven't done the assigned reading). They think they can avoid the embarrassment of admitting ignorance by using complex sentences and multisyllabic words, and by making vague, essentially meaningless assertions. I have yet to meet a teacher or professor who's fooled by this kind of scheming.

In government, the tendency to speak in vague and unclear terms is a problem of epidemic proportions. The passive voice is beloved by bureaucrats hoping to avoid embarrassment. ("Mistakes were made" is the quintessential example.) Government officials have an uncanny ability to speak around the subject. No one ever lies in government. The unfortunate delivery of misinformation and inaccurate data somehow just occurs.

Straightforward speaking does make one vulnerable; it gives others the opportunity to voice their opinions and/or withdraw themselves. The more direct one is, the greater the chance of being challenged or criticized or deserted. And sometimes it's worth being roundabout for the sake of being polite. But, at the very least, it's valuable to recognize when you're obfuscating. That gives you the chance to choose whether to continue scheming or to quit. Unfortunately, most of us don't recognize when we're obfuscating; we do it out of habit.

It's Time for Everyone to Come Out of the Closet

It's important to remember that almost everyone withdraws on occasion. Hiding, running away, and remaining silent are natural responses to embarrassment and shame. But pulling in is rarely effective in the long run. In fact it all too often backfires. The shy person gets labeled difficult or unapproachable or snotty or self-involved. Consider the case of Brian. Disappointed with his own performance at work, he started keeping to himself. He stopped asking colleagues out to lunch and made a conscious effort to avoid his boss. But Brian's behavior only drew attention to himself. He soon got a reputation as a snob.

The more one avoids difficult interactions, the more one becomes trapped in one's own private world. Real intimacy becomes harder and harder to achieve. Confidence slowly erodes.[8] Furthermore, you become fixated on your own emotional ups and downs, your own concerns and considerations. As you interact openly with fewer and fewer people, your perspective becomes increasingly narrow. You forget what you have in common with others, and you forget that others are just as anxious in life (and eager to pull in) as you are.

On the other hand, the decision to come out of hiding, to take center stage, to be up front can give rise to a sense of profound pride in oneself. Such pride usually leads to greater confidence, which leads to ever more effective acts of self-expression. In other words, being bold can initiate a powerful spiral of achievement.

The mere refusal to be shy, that is to say the willingness to be courageous, can also benefit society as a whole. When Katie Couric underwent an on-air colonoscopy in March 2000, she was certainly defying social norms. Many people wouldn't even tell their own families about getting a colonoscopy, never mind the entire nation. Couric's impetus was her husband's death as a result of colon cancer. She wanted to educate the public about the disease and the importance of routine colon screening, which was why she was willing to have her own insides broadcast on national television. Her decision had a major impact on society. A University of Michigan study of 400 endoscopists showed the number of colonoscopies increased 19 percent in the nine months after the show aired. Study author Mark Fendrick said, "Not only did

Katie's TV campaign have an immediate impact, but the significant increase in screening rates remained long after the broadcast."[9]

Katie Couric's courage potentially affected millions of viewers, but even the tiniest act of situational bravery can be inspiring and can initiate a spiral of achievement. My friend Charles told me recently about an experience he had in the Department of Motor Vehicles while waiting to have his license processed. A man sitting behind him was testing the ring volume on his cell phone. The man made his phone ring once, then a second time, then a third time. Charles kept expecting him to stop, but the man kept making his phone ring, steadily increasing the volume. Charles wanted to say something, but he was afraid of a scene. ("I didn't want to look like a twit," he says.) Charles is a scholar of medieval French literature who is not exactly comfortable with confrontation. He waited for someone else to say something, but no one did. Finally, Charles turned around. "I asked him if he could test his phone *outside*." At first, the onlookers stared at Charles in apparent shock, but the man said he was sorry and put his phone away. Then everyone burst into applause. "It was," says Charles, "like being the star in my own Nora Ephron film."

Boldness is the key to achievement. Without it, great achievement is all but impossible. Some day, perhaps, our schools will produce graduates who never withdraw, who never succumb to the spiral of shame. In the meantime, each of us must endeavor to be bold in the face of embarrassment, to be courageous in the face of possible humiliation. That alone allows for the achievement of self-satisfaction and self-respect.

* * *

Varieties of Withdrawal

Stage Flight
Quitting/Bench Warming
Shying Away from Setting Goals
Emotional Concealment
Circumlocution

Questions to Ask Yourself

What reasons do you give for avoiding social interaction at work?

What reasons do you give for not speaking in public?

What goals could you set that would empower you in both your personal and professional life? Who could you share those goals with?

What are you hiding from your coworkers, family members, and friends?

How could you use clear, concise communication to improve your relationships with others?

* * *

Seven Secrets to Avoiding Shame-Inducing Situations

How do you accomplish the most in your life? How do you maintain and expand your spirals of success? To put it another way, how do you avoid making unnecessarily embarrassing mistakes?

Here are seven principles for maintaining and expanding your spirals of success. If you follow these principles, you will avoid embarrassment- and shame-inducing situations. You will also achieve a high level of self-pride and self-respect. Having had the opportunity to meet and work with some of the most accomplished people in the world, I have had a chance to observe and distill basic principles from their achievement. Of course, there are exceptions to every principle. But for the moment, focus on the application of the principles themselves, not on the possible reasons you might have for ignoring them. These principles are invaluable in living a life of ongoing Self En-Couragement.

1. BE ON TIME.   It's mind-boggling the extent to which people are late. Being on time is one of the easiest ways to impress others, impress yourself, and live a peaceful life. Being on time is a critical element of self-discipline. It is no accident that so many training programs—ranging from basic training in the military to religious training in Zen monasteries—stress the importance of punctuality. Punctuality is a precondition for

Self En-Couragement. There are plenty of successful people who are rarely on time, but their lack of self-discipline limits their effectiveness.

I should know; I used to be chronically late. It didn't matter what it was: a class, a meeting, a date. I was perpetually behind schedule. As a result, I spent most of my life feeling ashamed. I'd rush into a meeting, cheeks flushed, ready with my apology. I don't know if others noticed how often I was late (I'm sure they did), but I do know how badly I felt about myself. I couldn't enjoy life because I was always worried about getting to where I was going or feeling bad that I hadn't gotten there on time. It would take me ten minutes after arriving for a lunch or dinner date to stop thinking about having been late.

I didn't use any fancy psychological tricks to turn myself into a person who is always punctual. I simply resolved to make being on time a priority in life. (I did, I will admit, buy a watch.) I started leaving a half hour earlier than normal. I started noticing how much I hated being early, as if it indicated I was unimportant. To deal with my own dislike of being early I started traveling with a notebook so that I could always have something to do if I got to my destination too soon.

Being late is an unnecessary habit that inevitably leads to guilt, embarrassment, and a sense of self-resentment. It takes a very real toll on the psyche (and has a very real impact on others). As you become a consistently punctual person, you become proud of yourself and experience less and less embarrassment. You also gain the added benefit of being able to demand that others be on time—without any self-consciousness about seeming hypocritical.

Being on time is essential to maintaining a spiral of achievement. The moment you start running late is the moment you know you are sabotaging yourself. You can think of being on time as the first step to living a life of achievement. Whatever your reasons for running perpetually behind schedule, they are only robbing you of your freedom to excel. When you start showing up everywhere on time, you will be on the path toward a life of consistent results.

2. STICK TO THE FACTS. Lying induces fear, namely the fear of getting caught. And, truth be told, most of us do eventually get caught. From a practical point of view, it's just not worth it. Telling the truth is far easier in the long run.

Recently, a number of philosophers have started to come to the defense of lying as a morally justifiable option. I'm not concerned with morality. Whether lying is right or wrong is, for our intents and purposes, irrelevant. What lying does is create unnecessary opportunities to feel ashamed. And I would challenge the most eloquent philosopher to feel no shame after getting caught in a lie.

Am I saying that you should express your opinions without restraint? No, not necessarily. Your opinions aren't facts. "That dress is hideous" is a statement of opinion, not an accurate description of reality. (Though it's a fact that you think it's hideous.) If you listen carefully, you can tell when other people want your honest opinion and when they don't.

The important point is, don't fictionalize events to cover your tracks. If the subway wasn't late, don't say that it was. The chances of getting caught in your lie are too great. (Someone else in the office may have seen you having a leisurely coffee without saying hello.) If you left the house late, say so and apologize. If you were interviewing for another job, keep your explanation vague but as close to the facts as possible.

3. **KEEP YOUR CONVERSATIONS RICH.** (*Stop the gossip.*) Self En-Couragers see every conversation as an opportunity to realize a dream or accomplish an aim. They are always thinking of new ideas for the future as well as concrete proposals that could be implemented in the present. If they have a complaint or criticism, they deliver that complaint or criticism with the intention of producing a particular result. Self En-Couragers don't waste their words. They cherish them as tools for transforming themselves, their associates, and the world around them.

The problem is, most of us spend our time talking mainly about other people. In other words, we gossip. We take great pleasure in talking and hearing about the flaws of others. Gossiping can even feel like a way of creating intimacy. But if you've ever had your gossip come back to haunt you, then you know how precarious that intimacy really is. And you also know how risky gossiping is. Gossiping is a surefire way to end up ashamed.

The richer your conversations, that is, the less filled they are with gossip and the more filled they are with creative ideas and concrete proposals, the better you will be able to maintain and expand your spirals of achievement. You will find that you have more time to get things done and that you get more done in the time that you have.

4. **KEEP YOUR WORD.** Self En-Couragers are "count-on-able." You know you can trust them to do what they say they

will do. If you want to be an ultra-achiever yourself then you must practice the rare art of honoring your promises *no matter what the reasons you might have for disregarding them.* Self En-Couragers keep their promises to everyone: to their superiors, to their colleagues, to the people they supervise, to their friends, to their family members, and to themselves. They don't let anything—not the weather, not the economy, not the political situation in Washington, not their feelings, not their moods—deter them from honoring their word.

Keeping your word inspires others and inspires you, and in doing so produces a spiral of achievement. By contrast, failing to keep your word leads to embarrassment and shame. No matter how good the justification you come up with for breaking your agreements, you will always experience a certain degree of guilt for doing so.

Keeping your word makes life more challenging, but it also makes it less stressful. When I worked for the school newspaper in high school, I was always behind deadline. So I have vivid—and embarrassing—memories of trying to avoid the editor of the paper at every turn. Any time I saw him coming down the hall, I would turn around and head the other way or duck into the nearest empty classroom. I was constantly in hiding.

Part of keeping your word is writing things down. You and I think we can remember far more than we really can. Names, appointments, procedures—sometimes people even tell themselves they can remember new phone numbers. If you don't like carrying around a pen and pad of paper, get a Palm Pilot. Or a mini voice recorder. Anything so that you don't have to rely on your own memory.

As you practice keeping your word, you will find it's not as hard as you think it is. In fact, if you start making a ritual habit of keeping your word, you will find yourself naturally making decisions and choices that support your ability to honor your agreements.

A common mistake people make when they take on keeping their word is to play small: to avoid making big promises so they don't have to worry about breaking them. But how can you achieve anything really great if you keep your promises small? Make big promises. Make it clear if you doubt your capacity to honor your agreements (so that you don't leave people feeling disappointed or deceived) and then give it your all. If you fail to keep your word after giving it 100 percent, you will not have any sense of shame or embarrassment. Instead you will be left feeling proud of your effort. Columbus promised Queen Isabella he would find a direct route to India. He failed, but he certainly gave it his all.

5. **Play by the rules.** Playing by the rules means doing things the way you know they are supposed to be done, even if you can see a way to do them "better." It often means surrendering to the will of those higher up on the corporate ladder. In a relationship, it means honoring the terms of that relationship. Playing by the rules means declining bribes, reporting lawbreakers, and following your conscience.

Playing by the rules doesn't mean forfeiting your right to ask for an exemption or your right to propose new rules. It does mean accepting a "no" when you get a "no" or at least being willing to be open about your defiance.

Playing by the rules is crucial to creating a spiral of

achievement. It enables you to be a team player and it shows respect for the opinions and beliefs of others. It has an upgrading effect on all of your interactional networks.

The more you play by the rules, the more you will come to appreciate the value of the rules as they are. You will also eliminate a major source of shame, embarrassment, and fear in your life. When we secretly break rules, we end up anxious, guilty, and generally stressed out. Playing by the rules is an easy way to keep our spirals of achievement from devolving into spirals of shame and guilt.

6. MAKE SURE YOUR BOSS (YOUR SPOUSE, CHILD, ETC.) WINS.

Mafioso Benny Ruggiero once said, "You never embarrass a boss. If you embarrass a boss, he kills you." For most of us, the risks aren't quite that high, but if you do embarrass your boss by making a mistake, it can be a humiliating experience for you too. That's why Self En-Couragers make an extra effort to do a good job if there's any chance of the boss looking bad.

A simple way to win at work is to make sure your boss wins. Do whatever it takes. Go the extra mile. Imagine you were the boss: What would the ideal employee do for you? If your male boss likes to shave toward the end of the day, keep a fresh razor and a can of shaving cream in your drawer. If your female boss often gets a run in her stockings, keep an extra pair on hand so she never has to go to a meeting stressed out. When you make sure your boss looks good, you'll look good.

It's easy to find reasons not to work harder than the next person: "My boss doesn't appreciate it anyway." "I didn't get a graduate degree to do photocopying." "It doesn't matter how hard I try; she'll make a fool of herself regardless." But when the boss wins, you win. The successful boss is much more likely to be generous, patient, and communicative with his or her employees.

This same principle can be applied to family situations. If you go out of your way to ensure the happiness of others, you will avoid unnecessary arguments and feuds. Don't wait to be asked to clean the basement or do the dishes. Think from the perspective of the other person. Then you will feel the kind of pride in yourself that will allow you to accomplish whatever you seek to accomplish in life.

7. STAY INFORMED. Self En-Couragers stay informed. They continually seek out information from a wide variety of sources. They stay abreast of company policies, personnel changes, developments in the field, new software, new Internet sites, local news, and national news. They also keep track of anniversaries, relatives' birthdays, important dates, and so on. They keep track of their own finances.

Being uninformed is one of the easiest ways to make the kind of social gaffe that leads to a spiral of shame. Violating a policy, forgetting a birthday, not being aware of a change in staff sets the stage for embarrassment.

Only a fool thinks he knows all he needs to know. And only an ass assumes he can remember it all. Write everything down in a place you can easily find it (preferably on computer so you can easily search for it). If your computer or handheld can be set to alert you when you have a meeting or an important date, take advantage of that function. If you need to download appropriate software, do that. Obviously, there will always be more to know than you will have time to discover or absorb, but chances are you underestimate your capacity to process new information. One of the keys to maximizing the amount of information you retain is pushing yourself to stay present. Notice if you start to zone out during conversations or while reading. If that's the case, catch yourself and "force" yourself to be present. Otherwise you're just wasting your own time and the time of another person.

As you increase the scope of your knowledge, you will be better able to maintain and expand your spirals of achievement. You will be more successful at work, at school, with your family, and in your relationships. You will also be better able to anticipate problems before they occur, so that you can prepare for them. Ultra-accomplishment begins with being aware of what's going on around you.

chapter 3 The Costs of Covering Up the Truth

Sara is a clinical coordinator at the Manhattan Eye, Ear & Throat Hospital. Her job is to assist patients who have macular degeneration, a form of progessive blindness. As patients leave, Sara routinely reminds them that it is unsafe for them to drive home. "One time I was telling a man he couldn't drive," recalls Sara, "and his wife said, 'Why not?' I was surprised. I explained that he couldn't see ten feet ahead of him. The wife was visibly shocked. She turned to her husband and asked, 'Is this true?' He just shrugged his shoulders. She was fuming. 'Now I know why you almost drove us right into that truck! I've never been so scared in my whole life.' He had been too ashamed to tell his own wife he couldn't see in front of him. He'd put his wife's life and his own life at risk because he was too embarrassed to be honest."

All of us have lied to avoid embarrassment or shame at some point or another. We've lied to our closest family members, to our friends, to our intimate partners, to our coworkers, to our employers. There is an episode from the sixth season of *Seinfeld* in which a character says to George, "I've been living a lie." George responds, "Really? Only one? I'm living twenty."[1] Sometimes it seems like lying is the only way to avoid getting chastised, laughed at, scorned, or rejected. But is it effective? To what extent does lying facilitate excellence and to what extent does it get in the way?

There are countless reasons for lying. People lie to get ahead, to protect the feelings of others, and (in rare circumstances) to escape immediate danger. College students report telling an average of two lies a day.[2] Psychiatrist Charles V. Ford, author of *Lies! Lies! Lies! The Psychology of Deceit,* speculates that people distort the truth in one third to one half of the statements they make. In a poll conducted in the early 1990s, 90 percent of the respondents confessed to lying on a regular basis. While some of this lying might represent pure villainy, the vast majority of the lies we tell are told to conceal embarrassing information. To hide a mistake. To prevent the discovery of a broken promise. To conceal a personal weakness or flaw. To hide a previous lie. In other words, as a protective strategy to avoid social disgrace.[3]

Most discussions of lying focus on the moral dimensions of deceit. When is it ethically justified? When is it immoral? We're not interested in such theoretical questions. We're interested in the effectiveness of lying as a protective strategy. To what extent does it work as an image-control strategy?

There have been many great figures who lied on the way to greatness. JFK and Martin Luther King both lied about their marital infidelities. Winston Churchill was a political pragmatist. Even, some say, Mother Teresa indulged in a few financial fictions.

I'm not going to enumerate all the potential advantages of lying in various circumstances because when we want to lie we are remarkably talented at coming up with all the reasons to do so. Lying needs no defenders; we are all masters at justifying our acts of deception. But from a pragmatic perspective, lying is problematic in three critical ways. First, it arouses the anxiety of getting caught. It is virtually impossible to lie without subsequently worrying to some degree about being discovered. That anxiety robs us of the simple enjoyment of living. Second, lying leads to miscommunication, misunderstanding, and loneliness. No matter how small the lie, dishonesty has a *dis*social, *dis*settling effect. Third, if discovered, deception almost always results in a disastrous loss of face worse than the loss of face it was originally meant to prevent.

Beyond these three reasons, dishonesty is almost inevitably shame inducing. The telling of a lie almost immediately triggers low-level self-loathing. Because, whether we manage to justify the lying to ourselves or not, we all have a fundamental disregard for those who don't play by the rules, who wantonly put their own interests above those of others. Even the tiniest "white lie" usually nibbles at our self-respect. Unless someone has explicitly said they would prefer to be lied to than to be told the truth, can any lie ever be fully guilt free? When we lie we become ever so slightly, or ever so greatly, ashamed of ourselves. Except in the rarest of cases, this twinge of shame is inescapable. And it can cause us to further act in ways that are contrary to our own self-interest. In other words, lying triggers a spiral of shame. That spiral can—and most often does—grow rapidly out of control.

Lying as an Ineffective Strategy

Interfearance

Lying begins and ends in fear. For the most part we lie because we're afraid of being judged (and of suffering whatever the consequences of such judgment). Not only is this fear based on a certain presumptuousness (does anyone really know how another human being will react to being told the truth?), it is also a hindrance to effective decision making. The fear of being judged can be overwhelming, interfering with one's ability to think clearly. I call this fear *interfearance*. Interfearance makes it hard to evaluate all the available options and to consider the consequences of a potential course of action. It's interfearance that makes it hard to see whatever advantages there might be to candor. It's interfearance that causes us to do things we would never do in principle.

There is a great story in the *Psychology of Lying* by William and Mary Healy, published in 1915, about how hard it can seem to be honest. A mother sends her daughter to psychoanalysis to deal with her compulsive lying. One day, the mother, sensing something amiss, picks up her daughter's purse, searches through it, and finds evidence that the girl skipped one of her sessions. The mother asks the doctor what to do. Should she make up a story about the telltale appointment slip falling out of the purse by its own accord? Or should she refrain from confronting her daughter and pretend as if the whole thing never happened? The analyst encourages her to be candid: to tell the daughter about digging through her purse. The mother is stunned. "I could never do that!" she says. From her point of view, honesty is out of the question. It would simply be too embarrassing to admit what she's done. Even though she wants her own daughter to be truthful, she dreads the thought of being truthful herself.[4]

The problem with deception is that it leads to greater and greater fear. For when you lie you must hide the fact that you are a liar. So your ability to think clearly and weigh the potential consequences of your actions is even more hindered. Chances are you'll lie again. And again. And again. Because no one wants to be known as a liar and because the chances of getting caught increase with each new omission, exaggeration, or outright deception, interfearance grows at an exponential rate.

At some point we usually come up with an elaborate scheme to justify all the lying to ourselves: "Lying's the only way to get ahead." "Everyone in our family lies." "If my husband weren't such a cheapskate I would never lie." Alas, the justifying doesn't ever eliminate the fear of getting caught, evidenced by the fact that we continue to lie to cover up our previous lies. All the justifying does is make it harder to recognize the extent to which we are becoming increasingly trapped in our own fearfulness.

Miscommunication, Misunderstanding, and Loneliness

Imagine the following scenario. John invites Jill to dinner. In the middle of dinner, John accidentally calls his date "Susan," the name of his former girlfriend. Realizing his mistake, he blushes. But he thinks to himself, *If she finds out what I did, she'll stop liking me.* So he tells Jill that he has a cousin named Susan and apologizes for the mistake. For the rest of the meal, John can only pay partial attention because he is busy thinking about how he will get himself out of the lie about his imaginary cousin. Jill doesn't know what's going on, but she senses something is amiss. As the dinner progresses, she feels less and less connected and eventually decides that John isn't "the one," though she can't quite put her finger on why. When John phones her the next day, she never returns his call. Normally, John would eventually stop calling, and they would both chalk it up to "bad chemistry."

The smallest lie can send a conversation off course; it can derail a relationship. It won't necessarily do that, but there is always a risk involved in being dishonest because lying makes you nervous and the resulting interfearance hinders your ability to think clearly.

Lying also makes you feel alone. The moment you lie you cut yourself off from the person(s) with whom you're interacting. You enter a private world in which you have only your own thoughts and feelings to guide you. Hence the liar's near compulsive need to confess to a third-party confidante. Of course, the act of confession exacerbates the fear of getting caught because it's impossible to predict the actions of the confidante. Thus, no number of confidantes can ever eradicate the sense of alienation caused by deception.

Disgrace

As if the fear of getting caught and the misinteractive nature of lying weren't enough to make it unappealing, the fact is that lying can result in a loss of face far worse than the loss of face it was meant to prevent. When you get caught lying, you end up looking *really* bad. Few people remember what Nixon did during Watergate, but we all remember he was a liar. Most Americans can understand why a middle-aged male would have a dalliance with an attractive twenty-something intern, but it's hard not to cringe when you see footage of Clinton saying "I did not have sex with that woman!" No matter what Clinton says or does he will never be able to entirely shake his public image as a man of questionable character.

America is the land of forgiveness, of second and third acts. But the liar who gets caught invariably has to contend with his or her own sense of personal humiliation, not to mention the resentment of others.

There is probably no kind of regret as acute as that which follows after getting caught in a lie. You don't just feel ashamed, you feel stupid.

Examine your fears of embarrassment. What are you really afraid the truth will do? Can you really predict how others will respond to the facts? How many more lies will you have to tell to keep up the façade? Most important of all, what psychic price will you have to pay for being deceptive?

The Trouble with Not Wanting to Get in Trouble

The most basic kind of lying is that which is done to avoid getting in trouble. Whether the inclination to lie to avoid getting in trouble is instinctual or learned, it seems as if every child eventually discovers dishonesty as a means of self-protection. When parents represent punishment, lying equals potential escape.

Those who are successful liars early on will be the most tempted to continue relying upon deception as a strategy for success. It won't matter if the actual chances of getting blamed for something in a given situation are low, when the fear of getting in trouble kicks in, a lie will come tumbling out.

For almost everyone, the possibility of getting in trouble causes a return to a prekindergarten kind of terror. The problem is that it is so easy to get into even more trouble simply by falsifying the facts.

Take the case of Ronald Reagan. After announcing his intention to lay a wreath at the Bittburg Cemetery in West Germany, Jewish groups around the world called the president's plans an outrage because Nazis had been buried there. Reagan, eager to defend himself against charges of anti-Semitism, told the press he could empathize with Jewish concerns because he had been personally involved as an army officer in the liberation of Jews from a German concentration camp at the end of

World War II. Whether Reagan's lie was a calculated attempt to deceive the world or a hasty fabrication concocted with little foresight, it was immediately recognized by the public as a fantasy. It was widely known that Reagan spent the war years in Hollywood and never traveled abroad. His statements only further undermined his credibility with Jewish Americans.[5]

It's amazing how creative we can be on the spur of the moment. Think about the lies you've told: "My calculator must have been acting funny. It does that sometimes." "I sent you a birthday card two weeks ago! Wait a minute, what's your zip code again?" "I know we changed that line in rehearsal; I remember crossing it out." Good lying doesn't take practice, it takes panic.

The fear of getting in trouble is a powerful fear. Sometimes, however, there isn't even a real chance of getting in trouble; there's just the possibility of being negatively judged. But even that can cause us to fib or fudge the truth.

His second week on the job, Barry needed to send a fax. Another document was already in the machine, but it wasn't going through. Barry took out the other person's document and inserted his own. Just as his document was going through, his coworker arrived on the scene. "You took my document out to send yours?" she asked. Her tone of voice was enough to trigger Barry's fears of being judged. "No," Barry said, "yours already went through." She inspected her pages. "Well, where's the printed receipt?" Barry hadn't thought of that. So he made his lie more elaborate. "I have no idea. I just found yours on the table. I assumed it had gone through, but maybe it didn't." His coworker eyed him suspiciously. From that time on, she made it clear she didn't trust him.

As children we learn there are "good people" and "bad people." Good people are kind, considerate, smart, attractive, hard-working, generous, courageous, and honest. Bad people are selfish, mean, dumb, ugly, stingy, lazy, cowardly and dishonest. Good people live happily ever after. Bad people get punished; usually they're killed. Every children's fairy tale is based on this duality. Since it's impossible to survive child-hood without doing something "bad," every child worries about falling into the "bad person" category. It's natural that as adults we would con-tinue to worry about being a "bad person." It makes no difference that as adults we know that "there is no such thing as being perfect." Our childhood perspective prevails. The slightest mistake can trigger a sense of intense shame. "Oh no, I *am* a bad person."

Perhaps nothing makes us worry about being "bad" more than lying itself. Which is why, after telling a lie, it's almost impossible not to keep lying, just to avoid getting found out. There is a famous saying: "It is easy to tell a lie, but hard to tell only one." That saying is remarkably accurate.

When Lizzie met John, a Southern WASP, she wasn't sure how he would react to her Hispanic background. So Lizzie decided to down-play her ethnic identity. She said she had "a few Spanish relatives on her mother's side" but made it seem like she considered herself "just American." Today, Lizzie realizes she prejudged John. But she feels she has to continue keeping her family life a secret just to preserve her im-age in his eyes. She knows there's a good chance of him finding out that she really is Hispanic, and she dreads the thought of him discov-ering her dishonesty on his own.

The only way out of this mess is for Lizzie to tell the truth, to "de-frost the facts." When you defrost the facts you take them out of deep freeze. We'll be talking about the art and science of telling the truth in detail in Part II.

False Promising

When someone asks you do something and you say you will, knowing you won't, that's a case of lying in advance. For instance, if Stephanie's boss asks her to clean up her desk and she says "sure thing" even though she has no intention of really doing so, that's a kind of lie. Or if

Nick's wife asks him to get the air conditioner fixed and Nick says "will do" but knows he won't, that's tantamount to dishonesty. Both are cases of *false promising*.

If you're like most people, you've made false promises too many times to count. At best, false promising results in a sense of sheepishness; at worst, it can result in deep dishonor. When parishioners complained to senior Catholic church officials about sexual abuse by priests, those officials routinely promised to keep pedophile priests away from children, knowing full well they had no intention of following through on what they said. Their false promising showed callous disregard for the value of honesty (not to mention for the well-being of the children involved).

In its effects, making a false promise about what you *will* do is no different than being dishonest about what you *have* done. It leads almost inevitably to self-disrespect and the anxiety of getting caught. You just cannot help but feel bad.

Being Different

If you've ever felt "different," you know how tempting it is to lie to blend in. You may have lied or wished you could. The sense of shame that comes from being "different" leads naturally to dissembling. Painful memories of adolescent awkwardness can make matters all the worse.

The desire to fit in is natural. In the animal kingdom, belonging assures protection and survival. The one who is different may be denied food or shelter or the chance to reproduce. Human beings will consciously or unconsciously modify their speech patterns, facial expressions, body language, and dress to mimic that of the group to which they seek to belong.

But fitting in often requires a certain degree of deception. It may be as simple as pretending you know something when you really don't. Or pretending *not* to know something when you really do. Some people pretend that they have more money than they do; some people pretend that they have less. Some people pretend they are more sexually experienced than they really are; some people pretend they are more chaste.

Teenagers are usually desperate to fit in. Bookish students will often try to play down their smarts. Exceptionally bright African-American teens will sometimes try to "act black" to avoid getting accused of racial disloyalty. We all know that boys will fabricate sexual experiences to seem macho and that girls will conceal theirs to avoid seeming "sluttish." Teenagers will basically do anything to avoid being branded uncool. There's nothing wrong with wanting to fit in. Really, who doesn't? But the lengths to which we go to fit in can rob us of our dignity.

One type of deception that is often used to fit in is *nonobjection*. A study of stepmothers has found that women who marry men who already have children will often fail to correct others who mistakenly think they are biologically related to their step-progeny. An offhand comment like "your daughter looks just like you" will simply get a "why, thank you" in response.[6]

Another, equally subtle, form of lying involves the use of *disidentifiers* to throw others off the scent. Before she officially came out, Rosie O'Donnell often talked on the air about her infatuation with Tom Cruise. Though she vigorously defends her comments about the sexy superstar, most gay activists feel that her remarks were intended to keep viewers in the dark about her sexual orientation.

The powerful influence of the desire to fit in was documented by psychologist Solomon Asch. Asch asked participants in a study to determine which of three lines was the same length as a fourth. When any one person did the task alone, he or she invariably got the right answer because the test was designed to be easy. But when a person was tested in the presence of others who collectively gave the wrong answer (as they were secretly instructed to do by Asch), the unknowing participant would often go with the majority. Though most participants were willing to diverge from the group in order to give the obviously correct answer, a substantial number went along with the majority and said two lines matched that clearly did not.[7]

You and I are easily ashamed of—and will readily lie about—a wide range of private issues, from ethnic roots to illness to sexual dysfunction. People who successfully dissimulate about their true identity are said to "pass." The phenomenon of passing has received considerable scholarly attention in recent years. Throughout American history, light-skinned African Americans have attempted to pass as Caucasian, Jews have attempted to pass as WASPs, gays and lesbians have attempted to pass as straight. Passing may involve more omission than outright dishonesty, but it can take a heavy psychological toll on the person trying to pass, which is one of the reasons so many psychologists emphasize the importance of coming out of the sexual, racial, ethnic or religious closet. The problem with lying to fit in is that it only ends up making us feel worse about ourselves. It's impossible to be proud of yourself if you are constantly pretending to be what you aren't. The shame that comes from this kind of existence not infrequently leads to alcoholism, drug abuse, compulsive sex, and depression.

Sometimes we're not embarrassed so much by ourselves as by those we are associated with: our friends, family members, partners, coworkers, and so on. In these situations, we worry about how our associates' qualities or behavior will reflect upon us. Often enough we lie to avoid "guilt by association."

Young children are easily embarrassed by their parents, especially if their parents are "different." When Jerry Falwell was growing up, he was deeply ashamed of his father's drinking. He didn't want any of his friends to know his father was an alcoholic. "I knew a lot of kids at school who probably didn't have the money we had, but they had very happy family relationships. Their parents, family, were all close together. We were always careful to cover up, to pretend we had the same thing, talk about it as if we did. I doubt if any of our friends knew that Dad had a serious drinking problem until he was dead."[8]

Julian is a gay lawyer who started dating a man who happened to be a "pet therapist." Though the two had a lot in common when it came to hobbies and interests, Julian found his partner's profession embarrassing. Whenever Julian mentioned his boyfriend, he described him as a veterinarian. It was a significant stretch of the truth, and it made Julian feel sheepish. More than that, it robbed him of his serenity. "The whole thing made me tense. I was embarrassed by the whole 'pet therapy' thing, but then I was embarrassed that I was lying. At some point we broke up, and I just hope I don't run into him when I'm with my friends. He would be really offended if he ever found out what I did."

Confidence Games

The feigning of confidence is a common practice, but it can easily result in a spiral of increasing insecurity. For instance, when someone in authority—a manager, a parent, a teacher, etc.—feigns confidence, those below usually will too. Those below will do their best to hide their own problems, weaknesses, questions, and needs. And when those below act calm, cool, and collected, those at the top feel only more pressure to project an image of perfection. The spiral of insecurity continues to grow until no one feels safe to be themselves.

Men, in particular, have trouble revealing their weaknesses. Boys learn early on that it is important to seem tough. In adulthood that translates into appearing as if you "have everything handled."

Sometimes, of course, a boss has to feign confidence to make subordinates feel comfortable. And sometimes subordinates should hide their insecurities because there's nothing that's going to make those insecurities go away anyway. But for the most part the feigning of confidence will undermine an interactional network. It will eventually lead to a dissocial situation in which communication is strained, stilted, or nonexistent.

Boasting is another form of posturing. It too is borne of a sense of unworthiness. We try to prove we are better than others: smarter, more sophisticated, cooler, tougher, more successful, etc. In his book of es-says, *A Way of Being,* the famous psychologist Carl Rogers recalls how, as a young fellow at the Center for Advanced Study in the Behavioral Sciences at Stanford, he would posture to win the admiration of his fellow scientists. "The Fellows are a group of brilliant and well-informed scholars. I suppose it is inevitable that there is a considerable amount of one-upmanship, of showing off one's knowledge and achievements. It seems important for each Fellow to impress the others, to be a little more assured, to be a little more knowledgeable than he really is. I found myself doing the same thing—playing a role of having greater certainty and greater competence than I really possess. I can't tell you how disgusted with myself I felt as I realized what I was doing: I was not being me, I was playing a part."[9]

Studies show two major advantages to being honest about weak-nesses. First, the open admission of weakness is appealing. People who are open about their flaws tend to be viewed as likable, worthy of as-sistance, and deserving of forgiveness. For instance, a person who ad-mits to being ashamed when asking strangers for money for a phone call is more likely to receive change than a person who acts nonchal-lant.[10] The admission of a weakness usually causes blushing, and blushing is itself attractive; the person who blushes is likely to be viewed in a positive light. Second, the feigning of confidence creates hypertension whereas the open display of weakness decreases heart rate and blood pressure, creating a feeling of calm.[11]

Some people, especially women, have difficulty being open about their confidence. They feign embarrassment to hide their actual self-assurance. It's not unusual for a woman to make a show of her own in-security in the way she speaks. "I'm so not good at this kind of thing, but don't you think maybe we should consider using a more diversified approach? I mean, I don't know, you guys are way better at all this than I am." Hesitancy, self-questioning, and a tentative intonation can all be used to create a gloss of insecurity. In the long run feigning insecurity can lead to self-loathing. How do you respect yourself if you're always pretending to be dumb or weak? The feigning of insecurity can also stunt the growth of a group. If no one in a group feels safe to express genuine confidence, then the group cannot set high goals for itself or maximize its effectiveness.

Both the feigning of confidence and the feigning of insecurity are a form of emotional deception. Like any kind of dishonesty, emotional deception is tricky if not dangerous. While the fear of getting caught may not be so great, the threat to interactional effectiveness is always significant and the probability of feeling lonely in the long term is very high.

The revealing of weaknesses and/or strengths is an easy way to strengthen an interactional network. It creates trust, intimacy, and connectedness. We like to know that those we are working with or related to are honest. When you allow yourself to be vulnerable, it makes others feel safe.

Truthfulness and Peace of Mind

Truthfulness is not an answer to all problems, but it is an answer to the problem of anxiety created by the fear of getting caught lying. Honesty stops the spiral of shame from growing. It imparts peace of mind and the comfort of knowing that one has no secrets, nothing to be "found out."

Deception takes work. It takes mental energy to remember the lies one has told, and time and effort to make sure those lies are not discovered. Truthfulness allows that energy, time, and effort to be put to better use.

A person known for telling the truth is called a person of integrity. Harvard philosophy professor Sisela Bok points out in her book on lying that the word *integrity* comes from the same root as the word *intact*. The *Oxford English Dictionary* defines *integrity* as "the condition of having no part or element wanting; unbroken state; material wholeness, completeness, entirety." When we have no outstanding lies, we feel whole.

Alex used to work for a nonprofit organization that gives grants to Jewish communities in Russia. One day Alex miscalculated the amount of money a community was meant to receive. He only realized his mistake after the check was sent. He knew his mistake would set the organization back several thousands of dollars, but he was too embarrassed to go to his boss. So he fudged the books to make it look like the grant was the right amount. After that, going to work was practically unbearable. He felt anxious, tense. Finally, he went to his boss to tell him the truth. "I still remember how nervous I was. And at first when I told him he looked like he was in shock. Then he yelled at me. I just took it. Finally he said, 'Okay, let's redo the books.' So that's what we did. Afterwards I felt like I could breath again. The guilt was gone. The whole experience gave me a new confidence in myself."

The more honest we are, the more proud of ourselves we become. That pride leads to confidence, which almost inevitably leads to achievement. Telling the truth from the start or "defrosting the facts" postdeception is almost guaranteed to generate a spiral of achievement. That spiral of achievement won't just benefit the truth teller, it will benefit everyone else as well.

* * *

Varieties of Deception

Fudging
False Promising
Nonobjection
Using Disidentifiers

Questions to Ask Yourself

What lies have you told that you are afraid of getting
in trouble for?

What promises have you made that you know you have
no intention of keeping?

When do you use nonobjection to avoid standing out
from the crowd?

When do you use disidentifiers to prevent the truth
from being discovered?

How would your life be different if you didn't have any
skeletons in your closet?

* * *

chapter 4 The Liabilities
of Lashing Out

The year before my stepfather died, when he
was ill, my mother decided to host a low-key Thanksgiving. I could tell
she felt badly about the last-minute preparations; Thanksgiving had always been a big deal in our family. But when I peeked in the oven, I
couldn't help but chuckle. The bird roasting in the oven was clearly not

a turkey; it was a good-sized chicken. "It is too a turkey!" my mother said. She wasn't laughing. "Let's just look at the package," I said. My mother could barely control her anger. "If you want to dig through the trash, be my guest!" Of course, the package settled the matter, and after a while, we all had a good laugh. The chicken was tasty, and so were the sides. But there'd been a moment there when I thought my mother was going to throw me out of the apartment. She was embarrassed to have confused a chicken with a turkey and felt ashamed about "ruining" Thanksgiving, especially since my dad was sick.

Psychologists have long recognized the link between shame, face-saving, and aggression. When we feel ashamed or embarrassed, we often act like the best defense is a good offense. The child who is humiliated by an older sibling will often turn on smaller classmates. The man who is ashamed of his meager paycheck may turn on his wife.[1] When Hitler came to power, he frequently reminded the Germans of how humiliated they'd been by the Treaty of Versailles. His aim was to make the Germans burn for revenge, and he succeeded. The Ku Klux Klan found support for its nefarious activities by appealing to similar desires for revenge in the defeated and humiliated South.

But one doesn't have to be a fanatic to lash out after an embarrassing incident. We all do it sometimes. It's part of being human. When we feel ashamed, there's always the temptation to get snappish, sarcastic, or short—to try to bully one's opponent or whoever happens to be closest by. It's a natural response to the experience of humiliation.

Intimidation isn't always a response to humiliation, but when it is, it represents a type of image control. Like withdrawal and deception, intimidation is a way of dealing with self-consciousness. The problem is that intimidation is very often misreactive. A says something to B, B takes it as an attack and lashes back, A is startled and decides B is someone to avoid. Few people respond well to being snapped at. Even if it seems like intimidation works (i.e., it produces the results one is seeking), it not infrequently triggers resentment, gossip, and backstabbing. Eventually, a habit of lashing out will weaken one's entire inter-actional network, meaning that there will be fewer people to turn to for support in times of need.

Sometimes, a sharply worded comment makes sense. If a male employee makes a sexist remark to a female manager during a meeting, it may be crucial for the manager to put the employee "in his place." Or if a student makes a homophobic comment, there's no reason for a gay teacher to swallow his pride. A quick verbal slap can make it clear that one is not to be messed with.

But all too often people lash out defensively without any aware-ness that that's what they're doing. They strike out in response to shame. In the late sixties, social psychologist Bert Brown conducted an experiment to test his hypothesis that human beings lash out when they're embarrassed at a long-term cost to themselves. Brown set up a situation in which opponents in a bargaining game were led to believe that they were being observed and judged by others. The best way to win the game was to cooperate; any hostile move by one player would end up costing both in the long run. But that didn't deter participants from getting hostile when they felt embarrassed. After several rounds, the participants were given "feedback." Some were told that observers thought they looked weak in comparison to their opponent; others were told that observers thought they were doing very well. When the bargaining resumed, those who'd been told they were being judged negatively used more vindictive strategies in the next round, even though those strategies came with a price. The results of the experi-ment were conclusive: When bargainers are made to look foolish or weak before an audience, they are likely to retaliate against the person who caused their humiliation. They will retaliate even if they know that doing so may diminish the chances of their own success. If you know you're starting to look bad, there's a good chance you're going to lash out, especially if you're being observed by others.[2]

Embarrassment-triggered aggression is a problem in many rela-tionships. The husband or wife feels guilty about something and gets snappish to conceal the guilt. Or one partner is embarrassed about a loss of social status and gets snappish without understanding why. Imagine, for instance, the following scenario. A man and woman are preparing to go to a party. The husband, who just got passed over for a promotion, knows that he'll be seeing an old friend, who now happens to be a prominent corporate executive. As they're leaving the house, the wife asks her husband if he wouldn't mind going into work a little late the next day, so he could help her decorate the nursery. Immediately the husband snaps, "You know, just 'cause your father was unemployed his whole life, doesn't mean I have the luxury of sitting around decorating nurseries." In such a situation the wife might conclude that her husband is a jerk, or she might begin to doubt his interest in having children. Unless they discuss the situation and all the factors behind the man's hostile response, the wife might never learn the real reasons for her husband's grumpiness.

Aggression is also a problem at work, where there is even less opportunity to discuss conflicts when they occur. It's easy to imagine a manager who feels ashamed for having miscalculated the budget snapping at an assistant who turns in a report with a spelling error. The problem is that the assistant is likely to end up resenting the boss for being difficult to please. Or imagine a receptionist, who feels embarrassed about having shown up late for work, being curt with a customer who calls on the telephone but doesn't know the name of the person he or she needs to speak to. The customer is likely to form a negative opinion of the company because of the rudeness of the receptionist.

Thomas Scheff is an expert on the relationship between shame and rage. Scheff, a sociologist, first got interested in the connection between the two when he was working as a marriage counselor in the early 1970s. Patients would come to see Scheff to deal with their anger, and Scheff, in what was then fashionable practice, would try to get them to vent their feelings of frustration. He would have them shout or pound a pillow or bang on a table. But, as he says, it never seemed to work. His patients made little progress. "I knew it was wrong, but I didn't know what else to do." Then one day Scheff began exploring the emotions *beneath* the anger and he found that his patients were usually deeply ashamed of some aspect of their own past behavior. Anger turned out to be a way of masking embarrassment. Once he helped patients recognize their own feelings of self-loathing, their anger toward others dissipated.[3]

Effective social interaction is impossible if one has no control over one's temper. The freedom to excel is only achievable when one has the capacity to think through the possible implications of one's responses.

Hushed Hostility

The relationship between embarrassment and aggression is rooted in the wiring of the brain. When we're embarrassed or aware of the possibility of being embarrassed in the immediate future, our brain goes into "fight or flight" mode. We then find a way to retreat or we go on the attack.

The leap from embarrassment to anger can happen very quickly, especially in children and, most of all, in children with Asperger's syndrome. Asperger's syndrome is a condition marked by sudden and sometimes violent mood swings, temper tantrums, and overwhelming feelings of rage. Brenda Smith Myles, an expert on Asperger's syndrome, says that embarrassment can send a child with Asperger's syndrome into an uncontrollable fit. Myles recalls an incident that occurred at a summer camp she founded for children with Asperger's. One of the boys passed gas during the showing of a movie. None of the other campers said anything, but the boy who'd passed the gas started screaming at the others. "He had a total meltdown," says Myles. "He started yelling and crying and lashing out at the other kids, saying they were making fun of him. None of the other kids even knew what had happened. He was afraid that everyone else was going to laugh at him, but the truth was the other kids were busy watching the movie. It was only when he began yelling about it that they started to wonder what he was talking about. That's when they figured out that he'd passed gas."

Psychologically healthy adults rarely lash out so directly. People are generally civil toward one another, at least on the surface. We usually suffer embarrassment in silence and then express our aggression in muted, socially acceptable forms.

For instance, lashing out can take the form of mild condescension toward one's peers. Kim Pettigrew, a sociologist at Auburn University in Montgomery, Alabama, conducted a study of female readers of romance novels and found that they all attempted to distance themselves from the "typical" romance reader. They would put down or express pity for other romance readers by drawing a distinction between themselves and their fellow readers.[4] Every woman Pettigrew interviewed said in one way or another, "I'm not like most romance readers." To quote one of her subjects:

> I find that I don't tend to want to associate with most other people who read romance, which sounds very elitist, but . . . occasionally I've picked up romance readers' magazines, *Romantic Times,* for instance, and leafing through this . . . it's just puerile, and full of adjectives and exclamation marks, and I'm saying to myself, I don't want to read this. And consequently, I don't want to associate with people who want to read this kind of thing.

By setting themselves above other romance readers, the women in Pettigrew's study managed to deflect their own sense of shame. As long as they could put down the "average" romance reader, the women in the study could feel sure of their own self-worth.

The condescension of one romance reader toward another is a mild version of the self-loathing/prejudice dynamic. Self-loathing often leads to prejudice and discrimination against one's own group, which leads to more intense self-hatred. Studies show, for instance, that men who are hostile toward gays tend to have repressed homoerotic desires.

Homophobic men are more aroused by images of male-male sexual contact than their more tolerant brethren. In other words, men with homosexual tendencies who are afraid of being rejected by their peers will save face by becoming outwardly hostile toward gays and lesbians. But their prejudiced attitudes then fuel their own self-hatred, so they become ever more homophobic.

The self-loathing/prejudice dynamic shows up in all sorts of daily situations. Imagine you make a mistake and your boss calls you on it. Then you say nasty things about her behind her back. Your own self-loathing has led you to a kind of prejudice, which has led you to gossiping. But most of us feel badly after gossiping, so we experience greater self-loathing.

The Sarcastic Sword

Sarcasm is one of the most commonly used weapons in social intercourse. It's an effective way of keeping others at bay. Sarcasm can cut down any opponent. The word *sarcasm* actually comes from the Greek "to tear flesh, to gnash the teeth."

Obviously, the occasionally sarcastic comment doesn't mean you're a defensive individual. Sometimes irony is just plain funny. Or a way of scoring a good, quick point. That's why we love Karen on *Will and Grace*. Sarcasm certainly helps when dealing with hypocrites and lazy minds. Think Dr. Phil. A little sarcasm can keep things light; I will use it in the classroom to get my students to take themselves less seriously.

But making cutting remarks can just be a crude form of image control. Then it's a way of saying "Don't mess with me; I can be very nasty if I need to." Sarcasm is often a shield, a protective device used to cover up a sense of failure. Very sarcastic people often turn out to be idealists and romantics who are embarrassed at having failed in the past to make their dreams come true.

If you find yourself being sarcastic, then it's worth asking why. Did you do something that you're ashamed of or embarrassed about? Is there something you're trying to hide or to protect?

As you start to look inward, you will probably find that what you've been telling yourself is funny isn't all that amusing after all. But that realization is useful. If you can tell the truth to yourself, then you can tell it to others.

The Trouble with Triangles

When we feel humiliated we don't necessarily lash out at the person with whom we're upset. Andrea may snap at Betty, but only because Andrea feels humiliated by Claudette. Betty may have no idea why she's being snapped at. Most likely she'll jump to a conclusion that Andrea is "difficult" or "rude." The relationship between Andrea and Betty will be permanently damaged unless one of them goes to the trouble of restoring trust and understanding. One of the most overlooked aspects of the embarrassment-aggression relationship is the triangular dynamic that is often at work.

Carl Semmelroth, a psychologist and the author of *The Anger Habit,* told me a story that illustrates the triangular dynamic. In Semmelroth's small Michigan town, there was a woman who wanted her lawn mowed on Fridays. The woman was a doctor's wife who generally entertained on the weekends. For a long time her gardener had come on Thursdays. One day the woman asked the gardener to change his routine. The gardener explained that he mowed the lawns of two other houses in the same neighborhood on Thursdays and that it would be greatly inconvenient to come back to the same neighborhood on two different days in the week. He apologized but said that if she really wanted her lawn mowed on Fridays she would have to find another gardener. The doctor's wife lost her temper. She called the gardener insolent and difficult. He was so hurt, he brought the matter up in therapy. Dr. Semmelroth helped him to understand that the woman was part of a small clique of doctors' wives in town and that she feared being rejected by that clique. The gardener's ability to assert his own independence seemed to portend further humiliation. She lashed out at him in a—albeit ineffective—way to save face.

When we're not aware of the triangular dynamic at work in a display of sudden anger, the anger looks personal. The gardener assumed the doctor's wife was mad at him for something he'd done when, in fact, what he'd done was only a minor part of the larger picture.

Ken, a sports trainer at a high-end fitness club, recalls dealing with a client who was clearly embarrassed about her weight. Like many of his other clients, she would wear oversized T-shirts and baggy shorts to hide her figure. (In this regard she was pulling in.) But she would also insult the other people in the gym, telling Ken how stupid they looked doing their workout routines. The woman didn't know the other people in the gym, so she had no real reason to fear their opinions of her. But she was worried about what her husband would think if she failed to lose the weight she wanted to lose. Triangulating her fear of embarrassment, she lashed out at her fellow gym members; their dedication to working out only threatened to make her look worse in her husband's eyes.

Victorious Victimhood

In its most subtle form hostility is hard to detect. It can even come across as naïveté or helplessness. In this form it has a certain pathetic quality. In the 1950s, psychiatrist Eric Berne, the founder of transactional analysis, discovered that everyday embarrassments can get translated into passive-aggressive game playing. For instance, the shame of having nothing to say can lead to a subtle kind of aggression that is easily mistaken for neediness. The person who has nothing important to say will often play what Berne called the "Why don't you/Yes but" game. In this game, a person will volunteer a problem in his or her life.

Others will then volunteer suggestions for fixing the problem, but in response to each suggestion the passive-aggressive person says, "Yes, but" and then explains why the suggestion is not going to do the trick. A "Why don't you/Yes but" conversation around the water cooler might sound like this:

A: I don't know what to do, I can't sleep at all lately.

B: You should try meditation before you go to bed.

A: Yes, I would, but it's so noisy in my building that I can't meditate at all.

C: Maybe you should try earplugs.

A: Oh, the noise doesn't keep me awake. It just stops me from meditating. No, my sleeping problems have to do with stress.

B: You could always have some brandy before bed.

A: Yeah, but my father was an alcoholic and that's exactly how he started drinking.

C: My wife had a hard time sleeping till she started going to therapy.

A: I would love to do therapy, but our health insurance plan doesn't cover it.

This game will continue until B and C run out of suggestions and find they have nothing to say. Eventually, one of them will switch to a new topic of conversation.

Why does A play this game? As Berne tells us, ". . . the real payoff is the silence or masked silence which ensues when all the others have racked their brains and grown tired of trying to think of acceptable solutions. This signifies to A and to them that she has won by demonstrating that it is they who are inadequate." In other words, the person who resents social situations because they are embarrassing ends up defeating all the others in the situation. The others feel frustrated because they cannot come up with a solution to A's problem.

Lose/Lose

Imagine for a moment that you're in a bargaining situation. It could be with your spouse or your neighbor or your boss. Suddenly you find yourself getting upset; you're trying to hold your ground, defend your position. You feel out of control, and the next thing you know you're threatening the other person with a lawsuit.

When we lose control of our emotions, we also lose our ability to think clearly and listen carefully. We can end up rapidly escalating tensions without even really meaning to.

Increasingly it seems, face-saving leads to litigation, or at least threats of litigation. When Oprah warned her viewers about the possible dangers of eating meat, the meat industry threw a stunning right hook: a multimillion-dollar slander suit. (The suit was a disaster: Oprah won in a legal and public-relations victory that made the meat industry executives look like a bunch of anti-American bullies.)

At one Ivy League school, a student from a very wealthy background was caught having cheated on his senior thesis. He'd bought a thesis from an on-line provider but forgot to remove the receipt that was stuck in the middle of the term paper. When his advisor accused him of academic fraud and said he would not be receiving his degree, the student, presumably mortified, got retaliatory. He announced that if he wasn't allowed to graduate on time, he would sue the university. Though he never followed through on his threat, the student, alas, had the right idea for our litigious culture: When you're embarrassed, threaten a costly law suit.

That kind of attitude may work in the short run, but it is destined to backfire over time. The accumulation of enemies can only result in disaster. Moreover, it's guaranteed to produce psychic stress. No one can cheat their way through life and then use legal blackmail without generating a certain degree of shame, which will only lead to further bad decision making and misinteraction.

The Embarrassment/Anger Spiral

Usually, our aggressive impulses are themselves embarrassing. So we end up in a cycle of embarrassment/aggression/more embarrassment/ and more aggression.

In the 1960s, psychotherapist Helen Lewis studied the transcripts of hundreds of psychotherapy sessions and found that patients were constantly experiencing shame, then lashing out with anger, then feeling shame over the anger. Lewis called these emotional cycles "feeling traps."[5]

The frustrating shame/anger cycle is vividly illustrated in a scene in Jonathan Franzen's novel *The Corrections*. Chip, a college professor, spends the night with Melissa, a female student. The next morning Melissa cancels her plans to spend the day with Chip in order to be with her parents. Chip feels needy and wishes his new paramour would choose him over her folks. But he's too embarrassed to say so; instead he criticizes Melissa's relationship with her family. In response, Melissa makes a dismissive comment about their sexual encounter. From that moment on, Chip becomes trapped in a cycle of embarrassment and anger. Franzen writes:

> Chip didn't ask her to explain. He was afraid she meant he'd been a lousy, anxious lover until he took Mexican A. He had, of course, been a lousy anxious lover; but he'd allowed himself to hope she hadn't noticed. Under the weight of this fresh shame, and with no drug left in the room to alleviate it, he bowed his head and pressed his hands into his face. Shame was pushing down and rage was boiling up.
>
> "Are you going to drive me to Westport?" Melissa said.

He nodded, but she must not have been looking at him, because he heard her flipping through a phone book. He heard her tell a dispatcher she needed a ride to New London. He heard her say: "The Comfort Valley Lodge. Room twenty-three."

"I'll drive you to Westport," he said.

She shut the phone. "No, this is fine."

"Melissa. Cancel the cab, I'll drive you."[6]

Melissa ignores him and opens the window curtains in order to survey the view. Chip grows angrier and angrier, but, being a modern, sensitive male, he transforms his hostility into withdrawal.

Chip dressed quickly while Melissa's back was turned. If he hadn't been so strangely full of shame, he might have gone to the window and put his hands on her, and she might have turned and forgiven him. But his hands felt predatory. He imagined her recoiling, and he wasn't exactly convinced that some dark percentage of his being didn't really want to rape her, to make her pay for liking herself in a way he couldn't like himself. How he hated and how he loved the lilt in her voice, the bounce in her step, the serenity of her amour propre![7]

Chip never does become violent. His anger triggers a period of self-loathing that ends in a deep funk of depression.

What's captured so brilliantly in this scene is the way embarrassment can lead to rage that only produces more embarrassment. Once this spiral of shame begins, it is excruciatingly difficult to stop.

Shame and Self-Punishment

The excerpt above raises the issue of a serious kind of shame spiral, the kind that leads to self-punishment through excessive consumption of alcohol, drug abuse, dangerous sex, and other kinds of self-damaging behavior. It's long been recognized that low self-esteem will often trigger a pattern of intoxication, remorse, and further intoxication that only leads to lower and lower self-esteem.

Intoxication is a way to escape, however briefly, feelings of inferiority. The man who is fired starts drinking; the girl who is dumped by her boyfriend starts getting stoned. Over the long term intoxication becomes a form of self-punishment as well. "I'm a bad person," says the self, "and the fact that I'm a drug addict proves it." So begins a cycle of shame and guilt from which it is harder and harder to escape.

What most people don't realize is that self-punishing behavior almost always reflects outwardly directed anger as well. The self-punishing person is usually filled with rage. Self-punishment is a way to cause others worry, grief, and guilt. In fact, what the self really says is "I'm a bad person *and it's your fault.*" Abusing alcohol, abusing drugs, having compulsive and/or unsafe sex becomes a way to make others pay.

The ultimate form of narcotic escape-cum-punishment is suicide. Suicide offers the same temptation as getting drunk or high: the elimination of feelings of low self-worth. It is also the definitive way to make oneself and others pay. Killing yourself is the ultimate form of lashing out. As if to make the point as vividly as possible, someone I once knew threw himself from the top of a building to the pavement below on his father's birthday. His anger was so intense that he thought it was worth taking his own life to make his father suffer.

Only Losers Lash Out

Intimidation is a dangerous game. The more you do it, the more others are likely to write you off. They will treat you like an acquaintance rather than a friend, they will stop telling you the truth about yourself, they will avoid working with you, they may even plot against you.

People who wish to be truly effective in life cannot afford to get trapped in the shame/anger spiral. That means one must be aware of one's own inclination to get embarrassed and to lash out in response. The key to handling shame-inducing situations effectively is what Carl Rogers called "being present." When you are present, you are able to notice your own reactions, no matter how slight or subtle. Being present makes it possible to choose a response thoughtfully rather than rely on a crude image-control strategy.

Defeating the shame/anger spiral opens up the possibility of greater productivity, greater connectedness with others, and greater self-respect. When one has the ability to respond to any incident (no matter how embarrassing or humiliating) in a relaxed, unruffled manner, there's no limit to what one can accomplish. Failures become insignificant; enemies become allies. Those who deal with shame-inducing situations gracefully benefit from their spirals of achievement. They are able to take pride in their interactional finesse, they gain confidence, they are less easily embarrassed and less prone to lash out, they gain greater pride in themselves, more confidence, and so on. Ultimately they acquire the ineluctable quality known as charisma.

Charisma is not something one must be blessed with at birth. It's a function of effective interaction with others. In the following chapters we will be examining the art and science of effective interaction, interaction that is not limited to the image-control tactics we mostly rely on. As we shall see, effective interaction requires first and foremost courageous engagement with others. The more courageously you act in life, the more you become proud of yourself and the more you become confident of your ability to handle difficult situations. Courageous interaction leads to accomplishment, which leads to further courage, which leads to further accomplishment. Ultimately, the spiral of shame and self-consciousness gives way to a spiral of achievement and success.

* * *

Varieties of Aggression

Snappishness
Condescension
Sarcasm
Triangulation
Playing the Victim

Questions to Ask Yourself

When do you lash out?

When do you use sarcasm to keep others at a distance?

How do you "play the victim"? Who has to pay a price for your victimhood?

What would you have to gain from being less hostile and more open?

* * *

PART II

Spirals of Success

chapter 5 Beyond Image Control: The Art and Science of Self En-Couragement

So far we've been looking at the ways we react when we're embarrassed or self-conscious. We've seen that withdrawal, deception, and intimidation are three of the most common image-control ploys as well as three of the tactics most likely to lead to a spiraling sense of shame and regret.

So how do you cope effectively with embarrassment? What can

you do to avoid misreacting after making a mistake? How can you turn a spiral of shame into a spiral of achievement?

Success in life begins with training yourself to be courageous: courageous in the ways you communicate with others, courageous in the risks you take in your personal and professional life, courageous in the ways you confront your own failures, your own fears, and your own dreams for the future.

In this chapter we will begin to explore the art and science of Self En-Couragement. Self En-Couragement is a practical way of building the skills of social bravery. It enables you to deal effectively with self-consciousness. And it enables you to transform your spirals of shame into spirals of success:

Self En-Couragement has three crucial steps:

1. *Deconstruct your beliefs.*
2. *Get the facts.*
3. *Take risks.*

Deconstruct Your Own Beliefs

Self-consciousness is always a product of belief, i.e., we believe we've done something to be self-conscious about. Self En-Couragers subject their own beliefs to rigorous scrutiny because they know that the human mind often misprocesses information. Deconstruction is the process of challenging your own negative self-beliefs.

Hard as it may be to accept, your interpretations of reality aren't necessarily accurate. You may think that what you said during the meeting was stupid. You may be absolutely sure. You may know it in your gut. But a wise person doesn't trust his or her own assessments of what's so. A wise person remembers that she is limited by her own perspective. Most of the time we are blind to the perspectives of others.

No situation is *intrinsically* embarrassing. The meaning of a given social encounter only exists in the perceptions of the people involved.

Self-consciousness is a sociosubjective phenomenon shaped by historical and cultural conditions. Consider the following example: We take it for granted that passing gas in public is embarrassing, but people in the Middle Ages didn't think so. They weren't ashamed to fart, spit, wipe their noses, or pick their teeth. They weren't even ashamed about being seen naked. Most of the things we today think are inherently embarrassing weren't embarrassing at all to medieval Europeans.

Embarrassment is a culturally determined phenomenon. There are wide differences in what is considered embarrassing around the world. In America, a person will likely feel self-conscious if stared at, whereas in southern Europe, people stare directly at each other all the time. In India, it's considered very embarrassing to have to give bad news. In China, it's especially embarrassing and shameful to disappoint one's parents. The British frown upon emotionalism; the French scoff at those who don't know their grammar; in the Middle East it's embarrassing to have to ask for help.

What makes a situation embarrassing or shameful, then, is that enough of the relevant people deem it as such. Who are the relevant people? They could be the person embarrassed, the immediate onlookers, the friends and family members to whom the story is told later. In some situations, it only takes one relevant person to create an embarrassing or potentially embarrassing context. For instance, when you go to lunch with your boss, you know you'll be embarrassed if you forget his wife's name, even if everyone else in the restaurant would sympathize with you that some people's names are impossible to remember. Embarrassment and potential embarrassment are always contextual, determined not by the substance of an encounter but by the context in which the encounter takes place.[1]

Self En-Couragers second-guess their opinions, especially when it comes to what's embarrassing. Imagine you get your profit-and-loss statement for the quarter; it says your division failed to meet target. Your first thought is *How embarrassing*. But what's really embarrassing about failure? That's the question to ask. Many of the most important and impressive people in history have failed. Lincoln failed to keep the Union intact without war. Should Lincoln have been embarrassed? Martin Luther King Jr. failed to end racial prejudice in America. Should King have been embarrassed? Why do we take it for granted that failure is embarrassing? Self En-Couragers question their own embarrassment. They interrogate their own beliefs. They deconstruct their self-assessments and opinions.

Obviously, deconstructing your own beliefs is not easy, because you think they are true. If you didn't think your beliefs were true, they wouldn't have any effect on you on the first place. So you need to play the role of scientist in your own life. Treat your beliefs the way a scientist would: Subject them to rigorous scrutiny. Conduct experiments to test them out. Write them down and show them to others. Go on the hunt for evidence that disproves what you believe. The ability to deconstruct your own negative self-beliefs is invaluable. Fortunately, it's a talent that anyone can develop. All it takes is sharpening your skills of skepticism. As it is most of us are pretty skeptical of campaign promises, religious epiphanies, and "new and improved" product claims. But we rarely turn our skepticism on our own negative self-beliefs. Every time you have a negative self-belief, you can ask yourself "Why do I believe that?" "What would an impartial observer say?" "What would I say if were a highly successful person listening to myself?" When you deconstruct your own beliefs, you start the process of liberating yourself from the spiral of shame and self-consciousness.

The story of Moses in the Bible is the story of someone who succeeded in deconstructing his own negative self-beliefs (albeit with God's help). Moses didn't believe he had what it takes to be a leader. He was embarrassed by his poor speaking abilities. (Biblical scholars say he had a lisp or some other type of speech impediment.) But Moses subjected his own beliefs to critical scrutiny and decided in the end that he was capable of being a spokesman for the God of the Hebrews. Moses managed to deconstruct his own sense of himself as incapable. That allowed him to be the courageous leader of the Hebrew cause and the one who would free the Hebrews from Egyptian bondage.

Consider a more contemporary example: When television producer Gary David Goldberg was casting the role of the cocky, conservative son on *Family Ties,* he saw Michael J. Fox audition but immediately rejected him. When they hit a roadblock, the casting director urged Goldberg to reconsider Fox. "Goldberg bristled at having his instincts called into question," Fox tells us in his memoir. Goldberg told his casting director, "'It's a waste of time, Judith. There's no way I'm going to change my mind on this. I'm a grown man and I know what I want and I know what I don't want. And I don't want Michael J. Fox playing Alex Keaton.'" Still, Goldberg agreed to see Fox again. Then, when he realized Fox was right for the part, he had to deconstruct his embarrassment about having been wrong (and having made a big deal about being 'a grown man' who 'knows what he wants'). In the end, he made a joke of it all. "'Judith,' he bellowed, 'Why didn't anybody tell me about this kid?'" Goldberg hired Fox, and Fox turned the show into a major hit.[2]

It's important to remember that at some point in life *you* constructed your own beliefs about what is and isn't embarrassing, what is and isn't worthy of self-consciousness. You may have had some help from your biological impulses as well as your parents, your peers, and society at large, but ultimately *you* were the one who constructed your beliefs about what's shameful, and *you* chose your arsenal of image-control strategies. Because of that, *you* have the power to deconstruct those beliefs and repudiate those strategies. That's something to be grateful for and to take advantage of to the fullest extent possible.

Get the Facts

A scientist who tried to find a cure for a disease without hunting down all the facts would be a fool. Same for a prosecutor who wanted to win a case. Or an accountant who wanted to balance the books of a company. Without the facts, it's impossible to do a good job, to have confidence in oneself and one's mission.

But in our personal lives we forget how important it is to get the facts. We trust our "gut feelings," our hunches, our moods, the opinions of our friends, the views of our family members. Usually we act like we have all the facts when we really don't. Say you get invited to a party, but you don't go because you're "sure" you won't know anyone there. Or you want to ask for a raise but you don't do it because you "know" your boss will say no. Or you want to ask someone on a date but you "know" you will get rejected. When it comes to what we think we know, we can be incredibly arrogant!

The facts are essential when making assessments about what other people are thinking. I will often hear people say something like "The other people in my office don't like me." Really, I say, how do you know that? Have you asked them? Have you done a scientifically valid survey? Or are you going on a "gut feeling"?

It's incredible how wrong our gut feelings can be. In 1928 most people had a gut feeling that the stock market would continue to climb forever. In 1939 Stalin had a gut feeling that he could trust Hitler. On the morning of September 11, 2001, most Americans woke up believing that it was going to be a regular day like any other.

The facts aren't always easy to get, which means it's a good idea to assume that there are always more facts out there to be gotten. Self En-Couragers are always on the hunt for the facts. They never presume that they have all the information that there is to be had. That doesn't stop them from making decisions, but it does stop them from becoming smug or self-righteous. (There's a certain self-righteousness to saying something like "I can't do it." It presupposes omniscient self awareness. A humble person says, "I don't think I can do it, but then again maybe I can.") Self En-Couragers are always willing to give up negative beliefs about themselves when the facts contradict those beliefs.

Victor is someone I would describe as an ultra-achiever. He produces results most people would find too incredible to believe. But Victor never thinks he has the skills he needs to accomplish his aims. So he keeps a detailed journal of his accomplishments. Whenever he has a doubt about himself, he refers to his journal. The journal provides him with the facts of his track record. It reminds him of what he has done in the past so that he can have the confidence to accomplish again in the present.

Self En-Couragers love the truth. They know that the facts alone can be trusted, but they are never complacent enough to think that they have the truth handled. They recognize that it is impossible for any one person to know all that there is to know, to see all that there is to see. So they maintain a certain perspective on their own beliefs, and they keep hunting for the facts. They live life in pursuit of the facts, knowing that it is the only true way to live.

Take Intelligent Risks

DOROTHY TO THE COWARDLY LION: *"Don't you know the Wizard is going to give you some courage?"*
THE COWARDLY LION: *"I'd be too scared to ask for it."*

—L. FRANK BAUM, *THE WIZARD OF OZ*

Ultimately, there is only one way to break free from a spiral of shame, and that is to take courageous action. Withdrawal, deception, and intimidation have in common a quality of cowardice. They are intended to protect against "hurt." The problem, of course, is that they usually lead to the exact kind of frustration and disappointment they are meant to prevent. So, transforming a spiral of shame into a spiral of accomplishment requires acting courageously.

Mostly we grow up thinking that courage is a quality possessed by only a few. We learn to equate courage with fearlessness. In movies and myths, the heroes are fearless. Superman is never afraid; given all his superpowers, why would he be?

But courage, as Aristotle pointed out over two thousand years ago, is not about being devoid of fear. It's about being unstoppable in the face of fear. The courageous person is the one who is terrified of diving off the cliff to save the drowning child but does it anyway. Courage is about smashing through the inner walls of self-doubt.

There are three different kinds of courage. The first is classic, physical courage, the courage to risk one's life or limb. The firefighter who races into a burning building has physical courage, pure and simple. The second is moral courage. Sherron Watkins had moral courage when she blew the whistle on Enron. William Lloyd Garrison had moral courage when he spoke out against slavery. The third, and least appreciated type of courage, is social courage. That's what we're interested in. Social courage can be as simple as asking for a raise or going to a movie alone or telling a partner about having been unfaithful. A socially courageous act has the power to halt a shame spiral. In fact, it can instantly turn a spiral of shame into a spiral of successful achievement.

Research shows that after you act courageously, you experience a transformation of your sense of self.[3] In the words of one scholar, acting courageously gives you a sense of "equanimity and contentment" and "an enhanced sense of personal integrity. There is an awareness that life has been lived in the best way possible, and there are strong feelings of self-satisfaction and pride." The courageous person has a sense of power, vitality, and joy and experiences being fully involved in life.[4] There are clear, long-term benefits to going beyond one's comfort zone. Risk taking increases one's sense of self-confidence, increases one's sense of power over circumstances, increases one's ability to manage anxiety and improves decision-making capability.[5] Best of all, research shows that, over time, risk taking becomes easier and easier. The more one takes courageous actions, the more one feels capable of doing so again.[6]

Maureen Neihart is an educator and clinical psychologist who systematically encourages her students to take risks and discuss their feelings about risk taking. "As youth have more experience with risk taking and also observe others taking risks, they begin to take more challenging risks. Their confidence and trust in themselves grow. The support they experience from others who are taking risks encourages them to take on greater challenges." She recounts the story of one student who, after engaging in risk-taking activities in class, decided to confront his father about his drinking problem. That conversation created a new, more positive relationship between father and son.

Being courageous does not guarantee real-world success. When Chuch Atchinson, a quality insurance inspector for the nuclear industry, blew the whistle on safety violations in the industry, he lost his job and was threatened with physical harm.[7] That was what he got for his courage. But being "cowardly," i.e., relying on tired image-control strategies to maintain face, is almost certainly guaranteed to lead to feelings of self-loathing and shame, whereas acting with courage results in feelings of pride and increased self-worth.

Being cautious may, in fact, be psychologically detrimental over the long term. One study found that young women who didn't take risks early on in life were more likely to panic or make poor decisions at critical turning points in their adult years. Getting practice in taking risks early seems to be essential for later success. People who don't push themselves early on tend never to develop a deep sense of self-confidence.[8] But pushing yourself produces the opposite result. By being courageous you increase your sense of self-worth.

Being courageous also has a positive effect on your interactional networks. Asking for help, telling the truth, and saying no give others the freedom to do the same. Courageous interaction almost always facilitates communication and generates collective enthusiasm. Courageous interaction is thus inherently prosocial.

Social courage is not for everyone. It requires a willingness to fail and to lose face in the process. Practicing the art of social courage is not for the person who would prefer safe, superficial encounters to rich, honest relationships. Honest relationships require a willingness to be vulnerable, open, and trusting. You have to ask yourself if you are willing to fail, to be vulnerable, to be open, to be trusting. You have to ask yourself if you are satisfied with the quality of your relationships now or if you dream of relationships that are more rewarding. No one else can tell you. You alone know the answer.

The meaning of "courageous interaction" is different for everyone. What is difficult for one person may be easy for someone else. You may find it easy to be emotionally honest but hard to speak up in public. Or you may have no problem asking for help, but you hate saying no. It doesn't matter. The key is to identify those areas in which you are stopped by embarrassment, shame, or self-consciousness and take the action you would normally avoid.

Ultimately, the socially courageous person stands to gain by *creating* face. Creating face is not something one can do by being cautious or pragmatic. It isn't something one can accomplish by relying on a damage-control ploy. The person who creates face doesn't win the envy of his peers; he wins their profound respect. Creating face comes from taking big risks.

In 1982, Coca-Cola's CEO, Roberto Goizueta, wanted to create a spin-off product to be called "Diet Coke." The company's lawyers fiercely opposed the idea. Never in its ninety-nine-year history had the company extended the Coke line. Company lawyers feared that bottlers of Coca-Cola would sue because their contracts promised them that no other product would bear the Coke name. Besides, they said, the company already produced Tab. Goizueta scoffed at these arguments. Thus was Diet Coke born. Some bottlers did sue, but that was hardly enough to stop Diet Coke from becoming the nation's most popular diet beverage.

Three years later, Goizueta took another gamble. Concerned that Pepsi was cutting into Coke's market share, Goizueta pulled the nation's most famous consumer product off the shelves and replaced it with a new beverage, named simply "New Coke." But there was astonishment and outrage across the nation. How could the Coca-Cola company so blatantly violate America's trust, critics asked. The backlash was fierce and intense.

But even this major blunder was a blessing in disguise. Only a few months later, Goizueta admitted defeat and brought back the original formula. The stock price jumped from 61.875 to 84.500, a 35.5 percent increase. By early 1986, the total value of the stock had reached an all-time high of $110 million. Goizueta was rewarded with over $5 million in bonuses. According to Coca-Cola's 1986 proxy statement, these bonuses were given for his "singular courage, wisdom and commitment in making certain decisions in 1985 which entailed considerable business risks, the net result of which has been, and will continue to be, extremely beneficial to the shareholders of the company." Today, New Coke is but a distant memory and Coca-Cola Classic remains the world's most popular soft drink. When Goizueta died in 1997, he was still in charge at Coke and one of the highest paid executives in the world.

There is an infinite number of courageous alternatives to withdrawal, deception and intimidation. Below I have outlined eight types of courageous interaction that are virtually guaranteed to halt a growing spiral of shame. For most of us, these strategies don't come naturally. They take conscious effort. But just as we normally select our interactional moves from our repertoire of image-control ploys, we can select from more effective styles of interaction. The point is not to memorize this list of courageous actions. Rather, this list is intended to provide inspiration and insight. Every situation calls for a different response. Use these suggestions to begin exploring new options in your life.

1. *Take the mike (Speak up when you'd really rather stay quiet).* Living a courageous life depends to a large degree on the willingness to *take the mike,* or in other words to speak up. Self En-Couragers are just as afraid of saying the wrong thing as everyone else, but they don't let

their fears stop them. They take the risk of raising a hand during a staff meeting or going to a teacher with a question or expressing an unpopular opinion at the dinner table. If they flub up, they keep going till they get it right.

Little children love to be heard no matter what they have to say. When little John Gottimer Jr. was seven years old, his dad ran for the New York State Assembly. His father was president of the Kiwanis, the Democratic Club, Hibernians, and the Holy Name Society, but nonetheless he dreaded public speaking. So when his campaign manager mounted a P.A. system atop his car and told the candidate to speak, Gottimer Sr. froze. But little John grabbed the mike and said, "Hi, my name is John C. Gottimer Jr. Please vote for my father, John C. Gottimer, on Election Day, last name, row B." Little John simply didn't know how to be embarrassed.[9]

Taking the mike is essential at school, at work, and, of course, in relationships. It means voicing whatever thoughts, suggestions, and ideas you would really like to share but would normally stop yourself from expressing. The key to effective vocalizing is saying what you need to say to the person you need to say it to.[10]

The virtue of taking the mike is that we all admire those who take the risk of expressing themselves. A young man in love would do well to play the role of Romeo and seduce his beloved with grand demonstrations of his affections no matter how ridiculous it feels. A would-be CEO could do worse than to speak up during meetings, even after making a fool of herself the first few times. Eventually she will garner respect for merely being willing to open herself up to criticism.

Taking the mike means resisting the temptation to withdraw into reticence no matter what the circumstances. It may mean saying hello to an unfriendly colleague or sending an e-mail update to an intimidating boss or sharing personal thoughts with an uncommunicative teenager. Taking the mike means putting trust in the power of communication to revitalize a relationship.

Some people prefer to speak up only when they have a script; they like to rehearse their lines ahead of time. Others take a more extemporaneous approach. Neither is the "right" way.

My Uncle Hans knew how to take the mike and he kept at it until he was in nineties. He would talk to anyone, anywhere. He would pay compliments to pretty women he saw on the street and tease clerks who moved too slowly. As a result of his audacity, he climbed to the top of his profession, never failed to get the best table in the house, and found a girlfriend forty years his junior. His boldness didn't make him enemies; it won him admirers. And he was just as afraid of public speaking as anyone else. In fact, when he was in college, he was asked to give the commencement address, and he panicked and fainted. But from that time on he was determined not to let his fears stop him, and they never did.

Taking the mike is valuable any time you find yourself withdrawing in a state of embarrassment, shame, or guilt. All you have to do is start speaking. What comes out may not be perfect or ideal, but it will keep you from going down the path of dissociality.

Admittedly, there are some people who talk too much. Others too loudly. They seem to comfort themselves with the sound of their own voice. Yet usually these "talkers" don't really vocalize what's important to them. They talk to *avoid* vocalizing, to *avoid* sharing themselves. They talk about the weather or traffic or fashion or the latest game. They often have opinions galore and make sure everyone around them knows their opinions. But they don't vocalize their fears or their dreams or their promises. These they keep to themselves.

Whenever you would rather withdraw into silence, it is almost always in your best interest to speak up. Withdrawal is the first step into a spiral of shame and misinteraction. Taking the mike reverses that spiral and enhances the prospects of interacting in a way that can facilitate success.

2. *Open your ears (Listen when you'd really rather not hear what the other person has to say).* Most of us are expert listeners—when we like what's

being said. But listening to criticism, complaints, and commands is, for most of us, a real challenge. The temptation is to get defensive or to stop listening completely. But that can only result in misreaction and bad feelings on both sides.

It takes courage to take criticism. It takes a willingness to grow, to change, to mature. Mostly we're interested in *proving* ourselves, so we have little interest in *improving*. But relationships fester when there's no opportunity for mutual coaching and critique. We can only be our best selves when we allow ourselves to be coached and critiqued by others. Not infrequently it's the people we least want to be criticized by who have the most to offer us in terms of insight.

Complaints, like criticisms, are not easy to listen to. But Self-En-Couragers *want* to know what others think of them so they can do their best job. In order to be a great leader, or a follower who makes a real difference, it's imperative to know the good and the bad. Diane Sawyer recalls: "I think . . . of Don Hewitt, the executive producer of *60 Minutes,* who said once, 'I love you. I *hate* that piece.' It was thrilling to be knocked down and affirmed at the same time."[11]

It may be even harder to listen without judgment to commands than to either criticisms or complaints. In our individualistic, rights-based, upwardly mobile society, being told what to do is considered demeaning. We take offense at the slightest implication of duty. But that only leads to a spiraling sense of shame and irritation. Employees grouse when the boss is "demanding," the boss gets frustrated and thus gets more testy, etc. In marriages, husbands and wives often end up resenting each other over simple statements like, "Please, don't leave your dirty clothes on the floor." Self En-Couragers, on the other hand, appreciate being given simple, straightforward instructions. They certainly don't waste time or energy wishing they were spoken to differently. They have the courage to show they can take orders without taking offense.

It's a paradox of social interaction that listening is most difficult when it's most important. But when you practice listening to criticism, complaints, and commands without getting defensive or judgmental, you gain the ability to turn a spiral of shame into a spiral of achievement. That's well worth the effort.

3. *Make clear requests.* If you were to make a list of all the things you want but have never asked for, what would it include? Now ask yourself, How long would the list be? A page? Ten pages? An entire volume?

Most of the time we don't ask for what we want or need. Then, ashamed of not having what other people have, we withdraw, lie, or lash out. Self En-Couragers, by contrast, ask for what they want. They know that the worst that can happen is that the other person says no. And the best that can happen is that they can get exactly what they want. When unknown actor Sylvester Stallone wrote a screenplay about a no-name boxer who goes up against a champion, Stallone dreamed of being the star of the film and believed enough in the picture to want a share of the profits. Even though his desires flew in the face of Hollywood norms, Stallone had the gumption to ask for what he wanted. To everyone's surprise, he got it. Two producers accepted Stallone's terms and *Rocky* (1976) went on to become one of the biggest movie hits of all time.

To be effective in making a request, one must be clear and precise. If you feel bad about making a request, or if you're afraid of hearing the word *no,* the tendency is to be vague or indirect. Sometimes, we're so indirect the other person doesn't even know they've been asked to do something. ("I have a meeting at three" is *not* the same as "Please don't disturb me for the next hour while I prepare what I'm going to say.") Successful people are clear and precise when they ask for something. They say what they want. They find out if the other person is amenable to fulfilling the request, and, if it's appropriate, they find out *when* the other person will deliver on the request.

Granted, to be effective at making requests you have to be attentive to the needs, feelings, and moods of the other person. There is a saying in the fund-raising world: If you want money ask for advice, and if you want advice ask for money. (Wealthy, successful people love giving advice, and they love being asked for it. The more advice they are asked for, the more money they will want to give.) The danger with paying too much attention to the needs, feelings, and moods of others, however, is that people are so easy to misread. You may think your client is in a bad mood when really she's trying to impress you with her seriousness. When a production company was raising money for my play, *Baptizing Adam*, one of the prospective donors left the theater during intermission. He didn't come back for the second act. Nonetheless, when we called him up and asked him if he wanted to support the project, he said yes and ultimately wrote us a check for $25,000.

Some people are good at asking for things except when it comes to *Asking for Help*. Asking for help reveals that you don't know something or you aren't skilled at something or you have some kind of "weakness." My friend Gabriella has a hard time asking for help in clothing stores. She is four feet eleven inches so it is difficult for her to find clothes that fit her. Sometimes she even shops in the children's department just to find something in her size. She doesn't like to ask for help because she is embarrassed about her short stature. But when she doesn't ask for help, she ends up spending twice as long in a store and often goes home empty-handed.

In the 1770s, the American colonies were desperately fighting a war against Great Britain. The colonists wanted to prove that they were capable of ruling themselves and defeating the world's greatest power on their own. But by any objective account they didn't have the resources. Wisely, Thomas Jefferson sought help from the French. The French agreed to support the rebel cause, sending money and troops across the Atlantic. Historians agree that if the colonists hadn't gotten help from the French, they never would have managed to win independence from England. The next time you need help but are reluctant to ask for it, think of Thomas Jefferson and the courage he had to seek help from the French.

4. *Go naked*. Going naked means stripping off your protective layers and plunging into the waters of life. It means revealing your weaknesses and flaws to the world. In practice, it means being up front, telling the bad as well as the good, the ugly as well as the pretty. It requires a willingness to be vulnerable, but the rewards are usually well worth the effort.

Gina, who manages the grant-writing department for a biotechnology firm in San Diego, sent out several grants that she knew were poorly written. Gina hadn't actually written the grants herself (the work was done by scientists on the company staff), but she'd failed to edit them carefully before approving them for release, which was part of her job description. She'd been swamped with other tasks and had treated the grants in question as a minor matter. After they were in the mail, however, Gina starting feeling ashamed. Her sense of guilt growing, she even considered leaving the company. Her boss hadn't even said anything, but that didn't matter. Finally, Gina went to her boss directly and said, "Jeff, I want you to know that I let you down by not maintaining high standards for my department. I approved the release of several grants that weren't ready. You can count on me to be much more thorough in the future." As you can imagine, Jeff was impressed by her candor and her sense of personal accountability. He assured her he had full faith in her work and was proud to have her on his team. When Gina left her boss's office, she had a renewed sense of enthusiasm for her job.

Going naked is especially useful when giving a public presentation. Whereas most people try to hide their weak spots when they get up to a podium (retreating behind platitudes, looking down at their notes, making up answers to questions they really don't know how to respond to, etc.), effective public speakers take a more open approach. Scott is a graphic designer. When he was just starting out, he landed a plum job as an art director for *Redbook* magazine. The job required him to redesign the magazine, which was something he felt confident about. But then he was sent to a sales conference to give a slide-show presentation to the advertising sales team about the new design. "I've always been a shy person, so I dreaded having to go." The meeting was in Bermuda, and Scott was so nervous he bought six new outfits just for the weekend. However, in preparing his talk he made a wise decision: Instead of just showing images he was proud of, he also decided to throw in a few blunders. "The sales force loved it, and I actually felt comfortable up there giving the talk. Instead of me lecturing at them, it became a friendly conversation. Afterward, my boss was ecstatic. She told me that I made her look great, and then her boss told her that he thought I was a masterful speaker 'without any ego.'" Scott had been so nervous and the presentation was such a success that he went back to his room and literally sobbed with joy. "I'd been dreaming of being an art director for a magazine since I was twelve years old. And here it was, I'd done it."

Though the term itself sounds a little silly, *going naked* is a practical way of achieving trust and gaining respect. A recent article in the *New York Times* reports that even Russian companies and businessmen, notorious for their dishonesty, are now using transparency to get ahead. A Russian food company that hoped to go public revealed in its initial prospectus that one of its principal owners had spent nine years behind bars. According to the *Times,* the move "paid off handsomely." The company raised $161 million almost overnight.

Barbara Corcoran is a woman who exemplifies the art of going naked. A powerful and successful businesswoman, she never did well in school because of her dyslexia. Now, as the chair of the Corcoran Group, a real-estate company worth some $70 million, which she founded, she makes a point of being open about what she doesn't know. As a reporter recently observed: "for all her drive, she has no airs. Because of her early difficulties reading, she is still unsure how to use certain words and she doesn't pretend otherwise. When speaking about her employees' trusting her, she asked, 'Is it *implicitly* or *explicitly?*' Her blue eyes stayed steady during her question, and she just as easily admits a mistake or gives someone else credit. Her example seems to work; in 2002, the Corcoran Group's sales totaled $4.2 billion."[12]

5. *Join the party or throw one of your own.* We've all experienced "wall-flower syndrome" at some point or another. You want to join in the fun, but instead you stay on the sidelines, telling yourself you will join in "when you're ready" or "when the time is right." But the longer you cling to the wall, the madder at yourself you get, till you eventually leave, dejected and disappointed.

The only way to break out of the spiral of withdrawal is to join in the party. When? Now. The only way to be an actor is to go on auditions. The only way to be a writer is to write and send your work to agents and editors. The only way to become a professional tennis player is to get a coach. The only way to do what you've always wanted to do is to do it. When? Now.

The older we get, the more entrenched we become in habits and routines. We become increasingly reluctant to try the new: to taste new foods, visit new places, consider new ideas, take up new sports, join new groups. As a result, we lose the openness and vitality of youth. I think sadly of my grandmother, who, though she is in relatively per-fect health and has friends who would like to go out with her, almost never leaves her apartment. She eats the same foods each day and watches the same programs on TV. She rarely even turns the channel to try a new show. In a way, she's just waiting to die.

The more we say yes to opportunities, the more opportunities we discover to say yes to. When you attend a party, you invariably meet people who are planning parties of their own. And I'm using the word *party* in a metaphorical sense. Every event you attend increases your chances of getting new clients, meeting recruiters, finding a romantic partner, expanding your circle of friends. Each new project you take on at work, the more you learn about what's going on in the organization as a whole, i.e., what opportunities there are for advancement. And, the more you say yes to life, the more alive you feel, just by getting out of your cubicle or out of your house.

Joining the party is one way to break out of the spiral of shame. An even better one is *throwing a party of your own*. When was the last time you organized a potluck picnic for your coworkers or a reunion for your extended family? When was the last time you formed your own organization or started a new group? Maybe you dream of going into business on your own or creating a nonprofit to improve the lives of others.

It's hard to believe today but Wall Street began back in 1792 when a small group of men met under a tree in lower Manhattan to talk about starting a business association. Their group evolved into the New York Stock Exchange. In 1863 a Swiss businessman asked four friends to help him start an organization to promote relief during wartime. Their collaboration led to the creation of the International Red Cross. And let's not forget that the Catholic church was founded when Peter moved to Rome and invited the other apostles to join him there. Could Peter have ever imagined how rich and expansive the Church would become? There is profound truth in Margaret Mead's oft-quoted comment, "Never doubt that a small group of thoughtful, committed people can change the world. Indeed, it is the only thing that ever has." And every group starts with one person saying to someone else "I have this idea. . . ."

You don't have to commit to changing the world, but Self Encouragement requires taking risks. It's the only way to accomplish great results. And risk taking means embracing the possibility of embarrassment instead of running away from it. The men who met under a tree in 1792 didn't know they would succeed in transforming American business. They had good reason to suspect they would just be ridiculed for their efforts, but they didn't let their doubts interfere with their aims. They took a risk and it paid off.

Granted, being courageous can lead to just the kind of embarrassment that ignites a spiral of shame. For instance, you decide to start a business, but you fail within a year. Some might say that's worse on the ego than never having started a business at all. I would disagree. Never trying is guaranteed to produce feelings of self-resentment and regret. On the other hand, there is a profound satisfaction that comes from merely getting into the game. In my experience, moreover, those who keep taking risks—regardless of whatever setbacks they encounter—ultimately triumph over their feelings of self-consciousness and at some point get literally whisked into a spiral of accomplishment. It takes determination at first, but dealing with obstacles gets easier and easier with practice, and in the end the rewards are innumerable.

6. *Defrost the facts.* As we've seen, lying is almost guaranteed to trigger a spiral of shame. You lie, you fear getting caught, you lie again. The shame grows until you dread getting found out and all there is to do is hope and pray no one ever discovers the truth.

It is never easy to admit having lied. There is always some loss of face. But un-lying makes possible the achievement of genuine intimacy and connectedness.

I doubt there is anyone on the planet who doesn't have some facts in cold storage that are waiting to be brought back to room temperature. But each of us thinks that our lies are more shameful than anyone else's. So we let the facts get colder and colder, until they are covered with freezer burn.

Fact defrosting means saying "Listen, there's something I need to clean up." It's the acknowledgement of one's own humanity, one's own imperfections. It doesn't require elaborate apologizing or explaining, just authentic communication.

The first year I was a counselor at Seeds of Peace, the famous program for Middle Eastern teenagers, a crisis erupted at the camp. During a coexistence training session, the campers were paired up in the gym and instructed to interview each other and draw sketches using information gleaned from the interviews to give a sense of the other camper. Afterward the campers scurried to dinner, leaving their drawings scattered over the floor of the gym. Most of the pictures were what you'd expect: a boy's face accompanied by a soccer ball, a favorite food, a fantasy sports car; or a girl's face accompanied by a cat, the face of a best friend, a can of Diet Coke. But one picture was different than the rest: It showed the face of an Israeli boy accompanied by a swastika.

Immediately there was tension in the camp. Who had drawn the swastika? Was it a challenge? A threat? Suspicion immediately fell on Laith, one of the Palestinians and a young firebrand. Laith had been provoking campers and counselors alike since his arrival. He often gave other Palestinians who were too friendly with the Israelis a tongue-lashing.

Laith never denied drawing the swastika. An emergency coexistence session was called. One of the trainers began discussing the symbol of the swastika and used the word *Holocaust*. A small Egyptian boy, nine years old, asked what the word meant. An Israeli was called on to explain. He began talking about his grandfather and suddenly started crying. Laith was enraged. "These are crocodile tears!" he said. "You didn't even know your grandfather. My brother was in jail for five years. Do you see me crying about it?!" The Israeli boy yelled back, then Laith marched out of the gymnasium, followed by the other Palestinians.

We, the adults at the camp, were not sure what to do. It seemed like Laith was too filled with hate to be interested in making peace. Camp came to a standstill. The staff debated the value of more coexistence sessions versus old-fashioned sports activities. Tensions began to flare among the adult facilitators about how best to handle the situation.

That night, an alarm went off. One of the buildings on the grounds had caught fire. It was the building that contained all the passports and all the money of the campers. Amazingly, none of the documents was destroyed. But discussion turned to sending the Palestinians back home before someone got hurt.

Then the incredible happened. Tamar, the small Egyptian boy who hadn't known the meaning of the word *Holocaust,* the youngest and sweetest of the campers, came to the director. "May I speak with you,

Mr. John?" he said. Then, when they were alone, the boy explained that he'd been the one to draw the swastika. He hadn't known what it meant, or it that it would cause so much trouble. He just knew it was a symbol associated with Jews. Tamar hadn't wanted to come forward because he didn't want to get in trouble.

When that little boy defrosted the facts, the entire mood of the camp shifted. Laith apologized to the Israeli boy for dismissing his feelings about his grandfather. The Israeli said he felt badly for Laith and his brother. An investigation revealed that the fire was an accident, caused by an old stove. Today Tamar is one of the greatest champions of Seeds of Peace. He speaks about Seeds and tells the story of the swastika at official events every year.

By defrosting the facts, Tamar benefited others and himself. Had he never come clean, he would have had to live with that secret forever. He would have ended up blaming himself for all of the camp's problems. Defrosting the facts eliminates the anxiety that comes from having lied. It stops the shame spiral before it can grow any further. And, not infrequently, it leads to remarkable results. Conflicts get resolved; misunderstandings get sorted out.

7. *When you mean no, say so.* It's six o'clock and the phone rings. There is a moment of silence and then the familiar sound of a telemarketer beginning a pitch. "Good evening, I'm calling to let you know about a new service from Allied long distance. Am I speaking to the person who pays the phone bills in your home?" You want to hang up, but something doesn't let you.

"I'm sorry," you say, "we're really not interested."

"Are you aware that you could be saving thirty dollars a month on your long-distance bills?"

"I apologize but this just isn't a good time right now."

"How much would you estimate you currently spend each month on phone service?"

"I really don't know. Fifty dollars? I'm sorry, I have to go." But it's too late. You've already invested a minute in the call, and now it's going to get harder and harder to get rid of the sales person on the other end of the line.

Saying no isn't easy, a fact that has long interested social scientists. Ellen Langer conducted a study to see how people would react to someone trying to cut in at a library copying machine. "Excuse me," the experimenter said, "I have five pages. May I use the Xerox machine?" A whopping 60 percent of the people asked allowed the experimenter to cut in.[13]

The problem with not saying no when you really want to is twofold. Either you end up resenting yourself for being cowardly (and the other person for being demanding), or you say yes without really meaning it, having no intention of keeping your word. Either way, the situation is sure to create tension.

Dr. Paul E. Adams, author of *Fail-Proof Your Business: Beat the Odds and Be Successful,* warns entrepreneurs that the fear of saying no can ruin the best-laid business plans. It's a subject he's written about in his nationally syndicated column for entrepreneurs. "I've seen many cases," says Adams, "where people starting out in business are afraid of offending everyone. Customers. Employees. Even real estate agents. And they don't realize what this can end up costing them in terms of real cash." Dr. Adams says this has a lot to do with business culture. "We learn in the business world to be 'positive,' to say yes whenever possible. It's part of the whole mindset. Sure there may be some risk of losing a good customer, or seeing a good employee walk out the door, but often the advantages of saying no far outweigh the risks." He says people who don't want to say no but know they cannot in good faith say yes, end up saying "we'll see." Adams laughs. "That's my favorite, 'we'll see,' it's a great way of avoiding responsibility." Adams points out that evasive answers like "we'll see" lead inevitably to confusion and frustration on both sides.

Steve Kaye is a California-based business consultant who has written about the fear of saying no for *Financial Services Journal,* the on-line magazine of the National Association of Insurance and Financial Advisors. "People hate saying no outright," he says. "So they just sort of blow each other off. Instead of replying to a request, they'll ignore the request. Maybe people think if they wait long enough, the other person will forget they're waiting for an answer." The problem is that timid silence usually causes the person who has made the request consternation, self-doubt, and possibly resentment.

Sometimes, the desire to be "nice" is so strong, it leads to outright dishonesty. When I wrote my first book—a guidebook for students hoping to transfer from one college to another—my co-author and I sought a blurb for the back of our book from a relatively famous woman who was the author of a best-selling college guidebook. We were students at Brown, and this woman happened to be a Brown alumna. On the phone she told us she would gladly give us a blurb and would get back to us in a few days. We waited for her phone call, but it never came. When we contacted her a second time, she repeated her promise to give us a blurb, and again said she would get back to us. This went on for several months. Eventually we realized she had no intention of giving us a blurb. She just couldn't bring herself to say the word *no.* I'm sure she felt ashamed, and I know we felt deceived.

The more you practice saying no when you really mean it, the more effective you can be in everyday interactions. That doesn't mean you should say no just to prove something; it means you should be honest with yourself and trusting of the other person. Even if someone judges you harshly for saying no, at some level he or she will probably be impressed by your straightforwardness. Either way, you can take pride in yourself for daring to be truthful.

When Chester Arthur was elected president of the United States, he was one of the least liked men in American politics. When he left office, he was one of the most respected men of his age. What happened? He went from being someone who never said no to his own party to someone who had the courage of his convictions. While he was in office, his fellow Republicans wanted to keep the "spoils system" in place. They wanted to prevent Democrats from passing civil-service reform. Knowing he was dying of kidney disease, Arthur threw political pragmatism to the wind and said no to his fellow Republicans. Civil-service reform was passed, and an era of vast corruption was ended.[14] Arthur ultimately earned the respect of Republicans and Democrats alike.

8. *Take responsibility for what you've done (and forgive yourself for it).* When was the last time you were the first to say "I'm sorry"? If asking for forgiveness is something you rarely or never do, chances are you're caught in a spiral (or multiple spirals) of shame. All of us act like jerks on occasion, and it takes not just maturity but courage to show humility and ask for absolution. A cowardly person will get defensive and insist on why he or she is in the right. Courageous people take the bold step of apologizing.

Skillful apologizing is an art. The skillful apology is direct and to the point, includes a full recognition of the damage caused, and ends with a promise that it shall never happen again.

Norman Augustine, chairman of the Red Cross and former CEO of Martin Marietta, writes in the *Harvard Business Review* about how company executives must apologize and take responsibility for blunders quickly and cleanly.

> Crisis situations tend to be accompanied by conflicting advice—with the legal department warning, "Tell 'em nothing and tell 'em slow," the public relations department appealing for an immediate press conference, the shareholder relations department terrified of doing anything, and the engineers all wanting to disappear into their labs for a few years to conduct confirmatory experiments. My experience has been that it is preferable to err on the side of overdisclosure, even at the risk of harming one's legal position. Credibility is far more

important than legal positioning. In the Exxon *Valdez* incident [in which an oil tanker crashed and spilled millions of barrels of crude oil into the waters off the coast of Alaska], the lawyers advised against admitting any guilt in order to be better able to defend the company's position. In the end, the company suffered a multi-billion-dollar jury verdict *and* a tarnished reputation.[15]

Making a heartfelt apology is rarely easy. It is embarrassing because it is, by definition, a loss of face. It's an admission of unworthiness. Whether or not apologizing will come with any real social costs (and often just the opposite occurs), we fear that our admission of guilt will be used against us. So instead, we try to hide our guilt behind an overly friendly, or sometimes just plain frosty, façade.

Not every mistake requires an apology, and an apology can make another person uncomfortable. Some bosses don't want to hear apologies at all. Some parents feel threatened when a child apologizes, as if the child were saying "I'm a failure." But in most cases, a heartfelt apology is greatly appreciated, especially one for an overtly aggressive act. Alas, those who are most likely to respond to situations by lashing out are also those who are least likely to take full responsibility for their behavior. If you can't remember the last time you apologized to someone for something, chances are you're actively engaged in hiding your guilt.[16]

When we do apologize, we often try to backtrack and conceal our guilt by shifting the blame onto someone or something else: "I'm so sorry I'm late; the cab driver took the wrong route" or "I'm sorry about everything; I never should have taken my father's advice." This displacement is a face-saving device, an image-control tactic that may work once or twice with the same person but rarely more than that. Still, some advice givers *recommend* displacing blame. They say it's a pragmatic strategy that dissolves tension rapidly.[17] Sometimes these books go as far as to advocate telling "white" lies. Personally, I think such a realpolitik strategy, while perhaps effective on occasion, is a bad idea as a regular policy. The self-disrespect that it engenders is sufficient to make it problematic.

The dangers of displacing blame onto circumstances beyond one's control are illustrated in a medieval Persian tale:

A king asks a sage, "How can an apology be worse than the fault?"

The sage replies, "Assume you do something wrong and then apologize. But your explanation is even worse than your fault."

The king still doesn't understand. So the sage pinches the king's ass. The king yells back, "Are you crazy? What are you doing?"

The sage replies, "Oh, sorry, Your Majesty. I thought I was at home and you were my wife."

Displacement, as the tale reveals, is meant to "make things right," but it carries with it the risk of making a major mess.

Taking responsibility for what you've done is an act of virtue in the most classical sense of the term. Taking responsibility establishes trust and generates intimacy. When you authentically apologize for your actions (without trying to foist blame onto someone or something else), you demonstrate faith in another's capacity to forgive. You effectively assert your trust in the power of human compassion. The more you take responsibility for your actions, the more others around you will take responsibility for theirs.

Once you've taken responsibility for your actions, you have the inalienable right to forgive yourself for what you've done. We are, after all, human beings, and human beings make mistakes, sometimes colossal ones. So you are entitled to forgive yourself, no matter what. But it's futile to try to forgive yourself if you refuse to take responsibility first. (How can you forgive yourself if you don't even think you're the one to blame?) Only after acknowledging to yourself and to others what you did (and the consequences of your actions) can you really start to forgive yourself. Once you do forgive yourself, you will free yourself from that particular spiral of shame forever.

Forgiveness isn't nearly as hard as it sounds. It begins simply by recognizing that feeling shame or guilt in the present for what you did in the past is counterproductive. Feeling shame or guilt in the present for what you did in the past is a way of avoiding the real challenge of taking responsibility for what you did and cleaning up any mess you made as a result (paying back what you owe, taking care of the person you hurt, etc.). When you both take responsibility for the past and forgive yourself in the present, you instantly turn a spiral of guilt into a spiral of greatness.

9. *Keep standing, even when they try to push you down.* One of the virtually universal effects of self-consciousness is that it stops people from standing up for what they really believe in. Self-consciousness causes us to worry about seeming crazy, weird, or just plain uncool.

Courageous people stick to their convictions even when others would consider those convictions ridiculous, absurd, or impossible. Walt Disney had to pawn and sell almost all of his belongings before he got his cartoon company off the ground. Distributors thought his ideas weren't good enough. Just imagine how different the world would be if Walt Disney had given up on his dreams of being a cartoonist.

Granted, there is value in listening to experts. I've had plenty of would-be writers send me manuscripts that needed lots of work before they would ever get treated seriously by an agent or an editor. But it's easy to overvalue the opinions of others. A mentor once advised me, "Get everyone's advice and then ignore all of it." His point was that the big decisions we make must come from our hearts, not our heads. Part of the reason I am tough on would-be writers is that I know that they will face harsh criticism throughout their career, so they ought to develop a taste for it early on.

The stories of people who have triumphed over incredible obstacles and vast opposition can be found in an array of inspiring self-help books. But my favorite is that of Abraham Lincoln, who faced obstacle after obstacle but never gave up his dreams. As a young man he made some bad business decisions but managed to overcome them, then ran for the state legislature and lost but tried again and got himself elected the second time. He ran twice for speaker of the Illinois House of Representatives, and, though he failed both times, he decided to run for the U.S. House of Representatives and won. He was twice unable to get enough votes to be elected to the U.S. Senate but nevertheless ran for the White House and won the biggest contest of all, becoming arguably the most important president in American history. And, of course, when the South seceded, Lincoln staked everything to hold the Union together.

There are two kinds of determination: the determination to follow through on a dream and the determination to be true to one's beliefs. Both have a way of paying off in the end.

Recently I met a woman named Miriam, who as a young instructor at an East Coast community college discovered that other faculty members in her department were scamming money from the state by reporting that they were teaching classes they weren't really teaching. As she started to investigate, she found that dozens of different people were involved in the scam. When the D.A. came to talk to her, she had to decide whether or not to blow the whistle. She did, knowing it could cost her her promotion. In fact, she was turned down for promotion the next year. But the year after that, she discovered, she was eligible for automatic promotion. She stayed at the school for twenty years, eventually acquiring a reputation as a woman of integrity and being promoted to department chair. Today, she is extremely proud of what she did. News reports of other whistle-blowers—like Coleen Rowley, who blew the whistle on the FBI, and Cynthia Cooper, who blew the whistle on WorldCom—indicate that standing up for one's principles is usually the safest bet.

Truth be told, you and I have strong feelings about how people should treat each other, but we mostly keep our opinions to ourselves (or only share them with our close friends). We don't want to be accused of being overly critical or, even worse, hypocritical. And we don't want to be held to account by sassy friends and family members ("I thought you didn't believe in supporting global fast-food conglomerates . . . ?") But the more we hide what we really believe, the less satisfying life becomes. And the less effective we become in our inter-actions. Hiding our true feelings makes us resentful, resigned, and im-patient. On the other hand, those who are straightforward about their values and observations advance both their own interests and those of others. Just think of a great movie director. A great movie director will let an actor know when he isn't giving his all. That benefits both the di-rector and the actor. The only way to be really fulfilled and effective in life is to be tirelessly true to your own values, and the only way to help others to be fulfilled and effective is to be as demanding of them as you are of yourself.

Being Courageous: A Brief Review

The three steps to turning a spiral of shame into a spiral of achieve-ment are: (1) Deconstruct the "Truth," (2) Get the Facts, and (3) Take Courageous Action. In this chapter I have outlined nine different ways of taking courageous action:

> Speak up when you most want to stay silent.
> Listen when you don't like what's being said.
> Make clear requests.
> Go naked.
> Join the party (or throw one of your own).
> Defrost the facts.
> When you mean no, say so.
> Take responsibility for what you've done (and forgive
>   yourself for it).
> Keep standing, even when they try to push you down.

These aren't the only ways to be courageous, by any means. But these are eight excellent ways to practice the art and science of effective social interaction. Remember, the point is not to memorize this list; rather it's to consider how you could take courageous action to transform your spirals of shame into spirals of success.

In the following chapters we will be looking at how we often misreact to circumstances in our daily lives and how we can achieve interactional effectiveness. We will be looking at how spirals of shame and failure can be converted into spirals of accomplishment and pride.

Real success in any area of life can be achieved through a Self En-Couraging approach to interpersonal effectiveness. That takes work. Image control strategies must be acknowledged and scrutinized. Spirals of shame must be recognized. Opportunities for courageous action must be identified and taken advantage of. A Self En-Couraging approach takes commitment and dedication, but the potential rewards are innumerable. Every interaction becomes a win/win occasion. A Self En-Couraging approach opens the door to educational success, rapid career advancement, and revitalized relationships.

* * *

Questions to Ask Yourself

What opportunities could you seize for speaking up?

When could you practice being open to criticism?

What are you not asking for in life?

What facts have you kept frozen for years? What would be the virtue of defrosting those facts?

What "parties" are you avoiding in life?

What are you willing to take responsibility for having done? What are you willing to forgive yourself for?

* * *

chapter 6 Work: Turning Awkwardness into Excellence

Karen was vice president of human resources at a software company. Because people were often laid off by the company, Karen did everything she could to curry her boss's favor. Whenever he asked her to do extra work, she complied. One time he asked her to baby-sit his infant son—on a Saturday. Another time he asked her to do research on breast pumps because his French wife couldn't find a pump that she liked. Karen resented the requests—she wasn't even paid extra for the baby-sitting—but she never challenged her boss. The thought of having to tell her mother she'd been fired for "being difficult" was too humiliating. Then, suddenly and without warning, Karen was laid off. All the extra work turned out to have been for naught. Now she was doubly embarrassed: on the one hand for being fired and on the other for never having stood up for herself.

Karen was unemployed for ten months. During that period she did some soul searching. She resolved to become a more courageous person, to stand up for herself and her principles.

When she landed a new job, again as a human resources professional, Karen was glad to have a fresh start. But her first week she discovered that the company planned to lay off a large number of employees. After reviewing the salaries of all the company's employees, Karen felt certain the president of the company was making too much money. She wanted to say something, but could she? It was only her first week on the job. Again she worried about humiliating herself. Chances were, the president would laugh in her face. Or worse. How embarrassing would it be to get fired a second time? Yet this time Karen was determined not to be stopped by her own fear of embarrassment. If he laughed at her, so be it. If she were fired, she would take pride in her own bravery. She asked for a meeting with the president. He agreed to see her, and when they sat down together, she told him, a Harvard MBA, that his salary was too high. She said he would have to cut his salary if he wanted his company to survive. After the words came out of her mouth, Karen didn't know what was going to happen. But the president just nodded his head. He agreed to cut his salary. Then she counseled him against the layoffs. He took her advice, the company survived, and Karen got a raise. Karen did the remarkable: She turned a spiral of shame into a spiral of success.

At work, it seems like everyone is engaged in image control: withdrawing, deceiving, intimidating. Ashamed of not knowing how or what to do, people avoid asking for help. Embarrassed by their own mistakes or failures, people lie to their superiors, their subordinates, their co-workers, even sometimes to themselves. (Karen told herself that being asked to baby-sit on a Saturday was not "really" so bad. Surely not worth quitting over.) Or feeling humiliated, they lash out at whomever is nearest.

Shame spirals are so common at work, they become part of the culture. They color attitudes toward "face-time," the way people ask for (or don't ask for) a raise, the way people who are new interact with those who are old (and vice versa), the way people talk about their lives outside of work, etc., etc. Shame spirals are a major cause of low productivity, lack of communication, team mis-spirit, and overall discontent. This chapter explores the different ways that a spiral of shame can be stopped before it grows out of control.

From Stage Flight to Star Power

One of the most common responses to self-consciousness in the workplace is stage flight. Stage flight isn't just avoidance of occasions requiring formal public speaking; it's withdrawal from the larger "stage" of social interaction. Whereas stage *fright* is something that really can't be avoided—when it hits, it hits—stage *flight* is a consciously selected strategy. It's an image-control tactic. Even the normally outgoing, extroverted person may become strangely taciturn at the office.

Stage flight at work takes many forms. One of the most common is not asking for clarification. The head of the department says, "I want to see the TPL reports from last year," and you have no idea what he's talking about. Or it's your first day, and you need paper clips. But you just feel awkward asking someone where the supply room is, so you pick up paper clips at the drugstore on your way home.

The mere act of saying hello to coworkers can be a challenge. Kathy is a buyer for the menswear division of a retail company. When the company moved to a new building, Kathy ended up with an office in the middle of a different division of the company. She didn't mind, because her new office was larger than her old one and had a better view, but she was terrified of having to introduce herself to her "new" coworkers. It wasn't until she realized that her own shyness could be misinterpreted as aloofness that she decided to make an effort to meet her new colleagues.

Of course, almost everyone gets shy when it comes time to give a public presentation. Study after study shows that people dread public speaking. And it doesn't have to be before a crowd of hundreds. The mere task of giving a presentation before a group of one's peers is enough to make most people anxious and some people sick to their stomach. Old bromides like "imagine everyone is in their underwear" offer little comfort. So people strategize and find ways to avoid public speaking, then resent themselves for being cowardly.

Often, of course, people do take on public-speaking opportunities. But instead of dealing with their own self-consciousness effectively, they try to hide it. Knowing they don't know what to say but not wanting to be up front about it, they start speaking in platitudes: "It's an honor to be here today." "We're living in a period of tremendous transition." "The company is committed to paving the way for the entire industry." We've all been to talks like this, and we all know how boring they are. Unfortunately, withdrawal behind a barricade of platitudes doesn't work nearly as well as most people seem to think.[1]

"Public speaking" can take many forms, from speaking to a large group to picking up the phone to call someone in human resources. When conversations turn to money, it doesn't usually matter how many people are involved. Lots of people get shy about something as simple as asking for reimbursement for expenses. And almost everyone has a hard time asking for a raise. Somehow there always seem to be reasons to wait: "My boss is very stressed out right now." "February is never a good time to ask for a bonus." "Joe P. just got a raise, so it would be better to hold off a few months before asking myself."

Sometimes these reasons are legitimate. But how often do people put off asking for—and possibly getting—more money merely to avoid the embarrassment of being told no? Some people would put off asking for a raise forever if they could, because the thought of being told "No, you're not worth more money" is so unbearable. Alas, raises rarely come to those who don't ask for them. It would be nice if employers conscientiously rewarded their hard-working employees by increasing their salaries on a regular basis, but that's not usually how it goes.

Even asking for smaller things can be difficult: a personal day, for instance, or a vacation. It's not usually the threat of being fired, demoted, or passed over for a promotion that gets in the way. It's the more insidious fear of being considered lazy or selfish. Sue Anne Morrow, associate dean of religious life at Princeton University, admits she's embarrassed any time she needs something from someone else. "I think of myself as very independent," she says, "so I'm embarrassed by my needs." At work, she is often reluctant to make requests.

What people don't often realize is that their practice of pulling in can be very frustrating for those above them. Admir Imami is a manager of operations at Merrill Lynch. He knows that the people who report directly to him often have things they want to communicate that they never do. "Sometimes it drives me crazy," he says. "Why don't they just come and talk to me? What are they so afraid of?" Withdrawal at work is usually misreactive. It doesn't produce the results it is intended to, and it can actually irritate superiors, subordinates, and colleagues.

For entrepreneurs and people in sales, the spiral of shame poses a serious problem, often getting in the way of success. Rachel is the founder of a company that sells financial advice, but every time she goes to make a "cold call" to a new client she thinks, What if they realize I barely know what I'm doing? Rachel knows intellectually that she is just as qualified as others in her field, but that knowledge doesn't stop her from fearing the worst. She admits that she could make twice or even three times as many calls in a day if she didn't sabotage herself with self-consciousness.

Stage flight is often the first move that inaugurates a nasty spiral of shame. Simon Sefaty, a professor of international relations at Old Dominion University, confesses that he has allowed his concerns about being looked down upon by his intellectual peers to stop him from sharing his intellectual discoveries with academics at other schools. "It's terrible. I never send out my books or my articles to my colleagues because I am always afraid they will think my work is no good. But if you don't send out your books and articles, you cannot get your work known in the field. That has held me back tremendously in my career."

Anyone can go from self-censorship to self-expression. The key is being willing to look foolish or, rather, remembering that those who stay quiet end up looking foolish anyway. Margaret is a woman who is terrified of public speaking. The first time she ever had to give a public presentation she got to the podium and then started to cry. To this day she feels sick to her stomach every time she goes to speak before an audience. But Margaret is determined to demonstrate that she doesn't have to be stopped by her fears. She forces herself to speak in public even when she would rather stay at home in bed under the covers. She has even chosen a career that requires her to speak in public on an almost daily basis. Recently, Margaret was honored for her accomplishments as a public speaker and inducted into the National Speakers Association, one of the most prestigious such associations in the country.

Philip Zimbardo, in his best-selling book on shyness, recommends role playing as a way to practice being courageous. I call this *visioning*. When you vision, you imagine yourself to be the person you want to be: fearless, important, powerful, easy-going, and so on. Whatever calls to you. A particular way to vision is to imagine that you are only doing what you are doing so that someday you will be able to write a book about it all. It doesn't matter if you've never written more than a school essay; if you can convince yourself that you're a writer at heart, then you can talk to anybody you want to just to get material for your memoirs.

Another useful suggestion for going from stage flight to self-expression is paying attention to your *red thoughts*. Red thoughts keep us from interacting. They are the thoughts we have like: "He'll laugh at me." "She'll think I'm crazy." "They'll talk about me after I leave the room." Red thoughts are a form of mental spam. They are messages that clog our cognitive in-box and make it impossible to think clearly.

As you notice and erase your red thoughts, you can replace them with *yellow* ones. Yellow thoughts begin with "maybe": "Maybe what I have to say is really important." "Maybe if I say hello we'll end up falling in love and getting married." "Maybe this conversation could be the most valuable conversation of my life."

From yellow thoughts it's a quick step to *green* ones. Green thoughts propel you into action. Green thoughts empower you to go for it.

Ultimately, the way to turn around the spiral of shame and withdrawal is to take center stage and suffer the glare of the spotlight. After a while you will find yourself getting accustomed to the warmth of the lights. And there's a good chance you will get recognition for your boldness. In the end you may never want to stop speaking up.

Help!

Not infrequently, when a problem arises at work that we don't know how to handle, we choose not to ask for help. We fear that asking for help will diminish our authority or cost us respect. But not asking for help, or what we could call "proving," is a dangerous habit. The person trying to prove something often ends up merely proving they should have had the nerve to ask for assistance in the first place.

In Eliza's case, a colleague at the literary agency where she worked went on vacation and asked Eliza to "cover" for her while she was gone. Fresh out of college, Eliza was new to the world of work, never mind literary representation, and she wasn't quite sure what was expected of her. One day Eliza discovered a writer's signature was missing on an important document. Her coworker hadn't left instructions about how to handle such a situation. Eliza didn't want to ask her boss, because she was embarrassed that she didn't know what to do. So she called the writer and left a message, telling him to come into the office to sign the document. The writer, accustomed to having documents sent to him for his signature, did as he was told but wasn't pleased. Eventually, the writer complained to Eliza's boss. Now really embarrassed, Eliza found herself having to explain how she'd gotten into the mess in the first place.

Since the midseventies, researchers have recognized that many people are reluctant to ask for help when they need it. Many people report they do not collect unemployment or welfare even when they are entitled to do so because they are embarrassed by the stigma attached.[2]

Being embarrassed to ask for help is actually a good thing, as long as one goes ahead and asks for it anyway. In an experiment on aid giving, a woman was presented to a college class as someone in need of help on a research project. In one scenario, she made her request with composure. In another, she feigned slight nervousness and "accidentally" dropped some papers and tried to pick them all up as she spoke. Students who witnessed her nervousness were far more forthcoming with offers of assistance on her research project than were those who saw her acting calmly.[3] Showing that one is a little embarrassed is charming; it suggests an appreciation of the rules of civilized society (namely, that one ought not to ask for help unless one really needs it). But, when we don't ask for help at all, chances are we won't get it.

Colin Gautrey is managing director of Help At Work, a consulting company that was created specifically to provide managers with advice so that they would not have to request it from their bosses or colleagues. Gautrey has been dealing with mid- and senior-level managers for many years. In his experience, the higher people are on the corporate ladder, the greater the sense of threat to their own image when it comes to asking for help. "Many [senior level managers] seem to be stuck with the value that they should know the answers. That makes asking for help very hard." Asking for help from more junior employees is sometimes considered out of the question. Gautrey says it's like "father [or mother] knows best": Senior managers don't want to appear ignorant or weak.

Age differences can also aggravate feelings of awkwardness. Since we generally assume that knowledge develops with age, when someone older needs to ask for help from someone younger, it can become a tense situation. "We build protective layers to our emotions as we grow old," says Robert Staub, founder of Staub Leadership Consultants and author of *The Seven Acts of Courage,* who has observed the dynamics of fear and image-control in the workplace for many years. "Children are highly courageous because they don't feel the same need to conform that adults do. As we grow up, we become less risk-taking and want to take the safe course. Social status is one means by which we strive to feel good about ourselves. . . . if I am older and a younger person has power over me, I feel a loss of status and it threatens my sense of self-worth."

Gender differences also can complicate asking for help. Women may not want to ask their male coworkers for help because they are trying to prove they are "good enough." Men may not want to ask their female colleagues for help because they are trying to prove they are "better." The same goes for racial and ethnic differences. An African American might be reluctant to ask for help from a white coworker because the former feels that he or she has more to prove. Sometimes the need to prove oneself is legitimate, yet other times it's merely in the mind of the prover. A woman may be much more aware of her gender than the man sitting in the cubicle across from her. A person of color may think he has more to prove than he really does.

Technology can create divisions—and exacerbate anxieties—just as surely as race or gender. People who don't feel comfortable with a new technology are often too intimidated to ask for help from those who do. Nancy has been working in advertising for over twenty years. When new software transformed her profession in the 1990s, Nancy knew she was falling behind the times. Her younger coworkers possessed a computer fluency that she felt she would never have. Loathe to admit her "weakness" to anyone else at work, Nancy learned the new software at home by herself. "I did not want the people I worked with to think of me as so old, like helping me out would be helping some elderly lady." It took her almost two and a half years to learn the programs on her own. In retrospect, she admits that she would have learned a lot faster if she'd only asked for assistance from her coworkers. And she no longer believes that asking for help would have made her seem weak.

People who did not grow up around computers often assume that learning to use them is near impossible, as if it requires some kind of knowledge that they're not equipped to grasp. Dale Wiley, a computer-support person who works for Computer Help, a company that deals in computer assistance and instruction, says most of his clients ". . . think not that their questions are dumb but that in some way they are." The humbling effect new technology can have on people can lead to a sense of humiliation when it comes time to ask for help. Yet older people can at least blame their technological ignorance on the whims of historical change. For younger people, especially younger males, history provides no such refuge. Young men are supposed to be computer savvy, which can make it especially embarrassing for a young man to have to ask for help. He may perceive it as a display of social failure.

Usually, asking for help is a relatively private activity involving a conversation between only two players. The sense of fear we feel is mitigated by this privacy. But when requests for help are publicized, the fear of embarrassment can be overwhelming. At one company, the tech-support people started compiling a weekly list of their top-ten callers, those who needed the most help with their computers. The list was meant to be used internally by the tech-support department to identify training needs. But news of the report leaked throughout the company. Suddenly, people who once called for help on a regular basis stopped calling completely. As one of the tech-support staffers recalls,

"I ran into a user who had not called for several weeks. She used to call daily. I asked her why the calls had dropped off, and she said she'd heard about the report, and was totally mortified that she'd topped the list most weeks."

Staub believes a culture-wide reluctance to ask for help can easily put a company at a disadvantage. "Workplaces suffer because people are afraid of doing the wrong thing. They think if they display vulnerability, they will lose their standing and respect with co-workers or those who work for them." But if people are preoccupied with their own image, it's hard for anything approximating team spirit to develop. What arises instead is a kind of misspirit. Put fifty people together who are all afraid of one another, and you end up with a dark comedy or something fairly tragic.[4]

When I worked for a nonprofit organization in New York I shared an office with a colleague. Based on my first impressions of her, I decided it would be better to stay out of her way. She seemed like the go-it-alone type with a knack for alienating others. But one day she asked me if I could give her some tips about talking on the phone. In that moment, my whole attitude toward her changed. I was honored to be asked for my advice, and my respect for her increased enormously. From that moment on, we became steadfast friends and regularly turned to each other for coaching and support.

Asking for help is an easy way to make a connection with another colleague. It may not work every time, but it's certainly a better policy than trying to go it alone. Asking for help is a way of showing you don't think of yourself as perfect. It's a way of saying "Hi, I'm human too. Can we be friends?" It's hard for anyone to turn down that kind of request. Obviously you don't want to ask for help so often that you become a bother, but personally I'd rather be bothered by someone needy than kept at a distance by someone who seems coldly self-sufficient.

One tip you can use to practice asking for help is to *focus on the physical sensations* that arise when you consider asking for assistance. Most of the time, we get stopped by physical sensations in our bodies:

a knot in the stomach, a sense of dryness in the throat. But we don't pay much attention to these sensations, or we think about them in the most general terms. Experts find that when you fully recognize the physical sensations you are experiencing as you experience them, they tend to disappear. So that knot in your stomach, if you focus on it carefully, may go away on its own.

Focusing on the physical sensations of your self-consciousness forces your mind to undergo a mental shift from left-brain mode to right-brain mode. In left-brain mode, you and I are highly independent, language oriented, and time sensitive. In right-brain mode, we are more open to connection, more visually oriented, and more relaxed. In right-brain mode it is easier to ask for help than it is in left-brain mode.

Another way you can bolster your courage to ask for help is to find role models who inspire you. Winston Churchill practically had to beg Franklin Roosevelt for help when England was under bombardment by the Germans during World War II. Elizabeth Dole, just after graduating from college, sought help and advice from a U.S. senator. The senator agreed to meet with her and during the meeting gave the young Dole professional advice. Dole took that advice and went on to enjoy a remarkably successful career in government.[5] Almost everyone who has achieved something of greatness has done it with the assistance of others. All you need to do is find a role model who inspires you to make the requests you know you need to make.

When Yes Means No

The flip side of being able to make requests is being able to say no to the requests of others. But most people hesitate before saying no at work. In fact, some people never say it. They use an image-control tactic called "just say yes."

I once led a workshop for a company in which I paired off the participants and then had each person ask his or her partner, "Could you please take out the trash?" The other person was then supposed to say no. One woman, a secretary in the organization, could not say no to her partner, even to the contrived question in the exercise. "I just feel too bad," Kathy said. "I can't do it." It turned out she could never say no at work and felt overwhelmed by her tasks. Because the members of the office always ordered lunch from one place, and others in the office were partial to pizza and Chinese, neither of which Kathy liked, she rarely got to eat what she wanted for lunch. I was hardly surprised when Kathy said she was unsatisfied and unfulfilled in her job.

In most cases, people are afraid to say no even though there are no real risks involved. (Of course, saying no *can* have real consequences. No one gets to say no to the IRS without taking the risk of going to jail. And it's always possible to get fired, demoted, or passed over for promotion for refusing to do what's asked.) Since people who say yes are generally thought of as more easygoing, affable, considerate, and so on, saying yes becomes a convenient way to look good.

The problem is that when you and I don't say no outright, we often still find ways to avoid doing what we've been asked to do—procrastinating, forgetting, making careless errors, etc.—that can quickly lead to a spiral of shame. Kathy said yes to everything that was asked of her, but she rarely accomplished all of her tasks. Her actions said no even if she said yes.

It's a good idea to keep a written log of everything you say yes to (as well as everything you say no to), so you can see if you are being genuine in your work relationships. Then you can review your "promise log" at the end of each day or at the end of each week. If you decide you are not going to be able to keep your promise you can inform the other person right away. You may find after a few weeks of keeping track of your yes's and no's that it would be empowering to say no more often. At first you will probably have to deal with the sense of self-consciousness that comes from saying no. But after a while, the mere act of saying no will get easier. Then you will be able to accomplish what you need and want to accomplish, and you will acquire a reputation as someone who does what they say they are going to do. That's well worth the awkwardness of saying no those first few times.

Telling Lies, Well That's No Surprise

Rick works for a record label. He has a reputation for being devoted to his job. Not long ago his boss asked him to head an interdepartmental web project. Rick wasn't interested in the task (he felt overwhelmed with problems outside of work), but he was too embarrassed to decline the opportunity outright. "I didn't want to have to tell my boss about my mess of a private life." Instead, he concocted a story. "I told my boss that I'd heard that a manager in one of the other departments really wanted to give the job to someone in public relations, and I didn't want to create conflict between departments." The ruse worked. Rick didn't have to take over the web project.

But what did lying cost Rick in the long run? How did it take a toll on his self-esteem? For a while, Rick was worried that his deception would be discovered, which only added to the stress he was already feeling at the time. And did the lie create tension between the two managers? We'll never know for sure, but it's a good bet it did.

Rick lied in order to maintain face. He was worried that telling the truth would diminish his reputation as a diligent employee. Unfortunately, employees feel forced to lie all the time. At work, impressing others is usually a top priority. That makes for a stressful and often deceit-prone environment.

Don't be fooled. We lie even when the real risks of telling the truth are limited. Robert Staub says workplace fear is usually unrelated to real economic concerns. "People in most of the companies we have consulted with are more afraid of looking foolish, of being shamed, of being chewed out, than they are of being fired."

Image control—the practice of trying to manage how others perceive you—is not inherently ineffective. Successful employees practice image control all the time: wearing the appropriate outfit, saying the right thing at the right time, doing what will please the boss. But our image-control tactics may be ill suited for the situations that befall us.

Ellie was a waitress at a restaurant. Her manager, Annette, was consistently late with the schedule, often calling Ellie at home to let her know she was expected to work that night. Though it didn't seem to bother the other waiters very much, Annette's last-minute style irritated Ellie. She decided to bring the matter up with her boss but was concerned about seeming like "a problem." To manage her own reputation, Ellie made it seem like a staff-wide concern. She told her boss that there was grumbling going on among the other waiters. The only problem was that her lie made her vulnerable to discovery. From that moment on, Ellie had to worry that her boss or one of her coworkers would find out she'd fudged the truth to suit her purposes.

Perhaps lying is not as necessary or as effective as we often assume it is. No one is perfect, yet everyone hopes to be viewed through the lens of perfection. Sometimes it's best to be known as one really is, no matter how flawed. Jason was at a party where he met an attractive woman named Ally. Afraid of what Ally would think of him if she found out he was unemployed, Jason lied and said he worked as a marketing executive for a movie studio. A few minutes later he learned that Ally owned her own business and was looking for someone with a background in marketing. Jason was furious with himself for not having told the truth. But he was far too ashamed to admit what he'd done, so he lost a potentially lucrative and satisfying job opportunity. Meanwhile, he felt much too uncomfortable to continue flirting with his conversational companion, so he excused himself and headed for the other side of the room.

It's remarkably hard to tell the truth at times. You and I have a tremendous amount at stake in seeming as good as (or better than) the next person. Some people reading this may even find it hard to admit that they ever lie. But the statement "I don't lie" is usually something of a lie.

Being the hypocritical creatures that we are, we tend to excuse our own lies with justifications and rationalizations but have little tolerance for being lied to by others. Rarely do we attribute a coworker's dishonesty to that all too human fear of being considered foolish. When we're lied to, we get indignant. The other person becomes treacherous, malicious, or, as if it were any better, a "climber." No matter how many times you and I have felt the tingling fear that follows a mistake—the fear that leads directly to lying—we are surprisingly unsympathetic when someone else is revealed to have lied to us. Usually we cannot wait to tell a third person about what happened: "Okay, listen to what George the backstabber did today. . . ." Some of us even take a certain pleasure in being lied to at work; the crimes of others confirm our darkest opinions of human nature.

Telling the truth when we don't want to can both increase our sense of self-respect and earn the respect of others. It can also create connectedness. Avrim works for a financial services firm. He told everyone in his office that he was planning on taking the Series 7 exam. But then, to his surprise, he failed it. "I wanted to lie," he says, "and tell them I decided at the last minute not to take the exam." But instead he admitted his defeat. "Somehow just telling people I'd failed let me get to know people at work in a way I never had before. People started sharing their failure stories with me. I ended up going to lunch with someone who'd gotten kicked out of college. I'd had no idea." Avrim's small act of courage turned out to have a large benefit in terms of developing relationships with coworkers.

You can find the courage to tell the truth by *focusing on the future*. Imagine you are named director of your division or voted CEO of your company or elected president of the United States. Would you want to have lies in your past? Would you want to be known as a person of integrity? Would you want to be able to count on yourself to do the right thing? Telling the truth now is the best way to practice for later.

Risky Business

Back in 1977 Alvin Zander, one of the pioneers in the field of group dynamics, published a provocative book on workplace teams that should still be required reading for managers today. After years of research on how teams deal with success and failure, Zander found that workplace teams will more often focus on maintaining or saving face than on accomplishing their aims. They will avoid challenging tasks, ignore criticism, and try to rationalize away their failures.

Zander provides several examples of face-saving in action. In one case, a manager criticizes a sales team at a meeting for making less profit for the company than any other team; the members of the team defend themselves by saying profit shouldn't be the measure of success. They say they should be appreciated for their effort, not criticized for their results. Zander finds such face-saving strategies silly at best, counterproductive at worst. He explains the central irony of face-saving efforts: "The actions usually taken to reduce embarrassment do little . . . toward ensuring a future success, and thus a group that focuses on lowering embarrassment will probably generate embarrassment again."

Zander illuminates the many mischievous ways groups manage to maintain face (at the expense of their own success). For instance, if a group fails to reach a specified goal, the group members may, in 20/20 hindsight, discount the merits of the original goal. Some groups simply refuse to set goals, so they can never fail. And others will set goals that are pie-in-the-sky high. Why? Because then no one can blame them if they fail to meet their aims. As Zander writes, ". . . some organizations seem deliberately to select unreasonably difficult objectives so the members need not be ashamed of a failure; they instead may be proud of attempting to attain an impossible end."

The ways a group can try to save face are numerous and limited only by the creativity of its members. Groups will blame external circumstances for their failures; they will blame each other; they will blame the system used for measuring results; they will "misremember" their original aims and will also misjudge their actual results. Perhaps most important for the freshman manager to be aware of: ". . . the more a group has failed, the more the members deny that they are embarrassed by its failures." This denial of embarrassment can only get in the way of collective growth.

Zander's main point is that efforts to downplay, deny, or disguise failure displace the more useful and productive aim of striving for better the next time around. In his research, Zander found time and time again that groups will spend their energies reacting (ineffectively) to their own embarrassment rather than developing new strategies for accomplishing worthwhile goals.

Image-control strategizing may be costing companies millions of dollars each year as teams get sidetracked from their real goals in the effort to maintain face. It may be a time for a new approach to leadership in which team members are encouraged to understand the dynamics of shame spirals and the costs that accrue when teams waste time trying to look good.

In fact, more and more organizations are adopting just such a new approach to team effort. These organizations have realized that teams can make or break a new project. In August 1995, Mobil Oil Corporation's Lubes Customer Support Center instituted an innovative team-building initiative, emphasizing personal development and self-awareness. Team members confronted their own feelings of embarrassment, shame, and self-consciousness. From there, they were able to take a courageous approach to reaching breakthrough goals. Within eighteen months, the company was achieving record levels of performance.[6]

In the future, organizational teams might readily recognize when they are slipping into a spiral of shame and take immediate steps to reverse course. In the meantime, you can make a difference in your organization by calling attention to those image-control ploys that don't work and by encouraging your colleagues to understand the dynamics of achievement.

CASE STUDY:
TEACHERS—TRYING TO LOOK GOOD

Every job involves risk taking. But if we look closely at one profession, we can see the extent to which fears of embarrassment affect performance. I have chosen to focus on teaching because of my own experience training teachers to teach well.

While most teachers don't like to admit it, they hate standing in front of a group of students on the first day of the semester. It's part fear of public speaking, part fear of being disliked by their students, part fear of making a mistake that would undermine their authority.

For some teachers, these fears evaporate over the course of a term. As students reveal their own weaknesses, teachers tend to experience greater confidence and comfort. But for others, especially those who worry about their own qualifications, every day can feel like the first. Georgia Nugent, director of the McGraw Center for Teaching and Learning at Princeton University, says that the fear of embarrassment is a serious impediment to pedagogic effectiveness at the university level. Professors often fear that as students get to know them their intellectual weaknesses and pretensions will become appararent. She tells a story of a professor who came to the center with an envelope containing all the reviews he'd ever received from students. "I can't bring myself to look at these," he said with a flinch. "Please tell me if they're terrible." In fact, they turned out to be quite good.

(Alas, few college professors ever seek out assistance from university teaching centers, making the task of those centers all the more difficult. Most professors are loathe to think of themselves as teachers. Higher education in the United States is based on the principle that scholarship is important and that teaching is a necessary imposition to pay the bills. Prestigious professors often demand to be exempted from teaching duties. Having to teach is, in and of itself, considered disgraceful. Obviously, not all professors look down on teaching, and some even enjoy it. But the shame and embarrassment attached to "being a teacher" makes it hard for college professors to get interested in improving their teaching skills.)

The fear of "exposure" limits teachers' ability to communicate effectively. Some cannot look their students in the eye when they lecture. Many read straight from their notes. Some mumble. Others stutter. Some never give students an opportunity to ask questions at the end of a lecture. How many teachers conduct their classrooms like true conversations in which students can freely contribute their thoughts and feelings?

Unfortunately, the more teachers strive to prove their merit, the more students will do the same. The result is an educational system (especially at the university level) in which students often feel like they must pretend to be more knowledgeable than they really are. Says Nugent, "Teachers feel that they have to have authority. If they make a mistake, they fear they are going to lose their authority. They see themselves as exposed. One of the first things we tell beginning teachers is that it's important to admit what you don't know. You're modeling learning. If you want your students to admit that they don't know things, then you have do it yourself. It's important to be able to admit that you're not God."

I recently advised a college student who was afraid of asking for help from a professor to keep in mind that her professors were equally afraid of her. "How can that be?" she said. "They all seem so important. They don't even look at you in the hallway when you pass by them." I tried to explain that professors often avoid eye contact because they're afraid of being embarrassed by not recognzing a student or not knowing a student's name. The young woman found this too hard to believe. But it's true: Some professors disguise their social fears with absent-mindedness, arrogance, indifference, and occasionally hostility.

Teachers would do well to think of themselves as managers, and managers would benefit by remembering that they themselves are often teachers. To teach well, you have to put yourself in the shoes of your students. You have to remind yourself what it feels like to be the one who doesn't know, to have all the questions and none of the answers. Teaching (and managing) requires courage: the courage to be at one and the same time vulnerable and demanding.

Stopping the Buck

Sometimes it seems that managers are determined to create a climate of anxiety. One way is to publicly embarrass employees. This kind of control style is certainly disappearing, but it still exists in some sectors, especially in mostly male environments like Wall Street. Even in "softer" professions, like architecture, public embarrassment may be considered part of the game. Architects and artists, in fact, learn the skill of embarrassing others in graduate school, where "crit" is still a common practice. In "crit" the professor will have a group of students publicly tear apart one person's work for the alleged benefit of all.

People who work in organizations where public criticism is common tend, not surprisingly, to be especially cautious about revealing their true selves. They develop elaborate strategies to hide their weaknesses and avoid having to ask questions. In such organizations, secrecy and distrust usually prevail. Unfortunately, managers can create a chilly climate by being anything other than 100 percent open to hearing criticism. The slightest defensiveness can have a chilling effect on organizational culture. Sharon is the director of a consulting company. She has many strengths but also certain weaknesses. Her biggest weakness is being unable to acknowledge her weaknesses. For instance, Sharon is not very good at managing staff meetings. In fact, most staff members have come to resent staff meetings as a waste of time. But when Verna, a senior staffer, gingerly suggested at an executive committee meeting a new approach to the all-staff meetings, Sharon turned the situation into an are-you-with-me-or-against-me dynamic: "Are you saying people think I'm terrible at running staff meetings?" she asked. Verna hardly wanted to say "Yes, Sharon, the entire staff is on the verge of revolt." So instead she said, "No, it's not like that. I just thought it might be a good idea if we started using an agenda." "Well, Verna, maybe you're right," said Sharon cooly. "What does everyone else think?" At that point, no one else wanted to be on Verna's side, so even though they all agreed the staff meetings needed reform, not one of them came to Verna's defense.

Even if managers are not busy creating anxiety, they may be modeling unproductive hesitancy. Just as most employees dislike asking for more money, many managers are reluctant to ask for what they want from their staff. They may unintentionally set goals that are too vague or fail to check up on the progress of their subordinates. They may not mention an account executive's habit of showing up late for work or the receptionist's tendency to be abrasive on the phone. This sort of timidity usually stems from a desire to be liked. What managers don't often realize is that their hesitancy tends to be resented by those employees who are working hard and following the rules. Part of the job of a leader is to demand the best from everyone.

So what's a manager who wants to encourage openness to do?

Well, put simply, be open. Managers can set the example. They can admit when they make mistakes, confess when they've lied, initiate dialogue, ask for help when they need it, demand the best from everyone.

There are numerous occasions on which managers can encourage subordinates to feel comfortable and at ease. During the initial job interview, managers can talk about their own successes and failures. When an employee shows up for her first day, some managers share revealing stories from their own first days of work at the company. After a big failure of some sort, the conscientious manager might schedule a meeting to make sure the employee doesn't decide to give up, to provide suggestions for the future, and to offer encouragement. The more managers and employees are open and honest with each other, the more an organization will thrive. The manager who can make his employees feel truly at ease, even in the worst of times, is the manager who will ultimately win praise, admiration, and respect.

And what about those who are not in a position of authority? Is it possible for someone on the bottom to change the culture of an organization? In many cases, yes. The first thing those on the bottom can do is recognize their own shame spirals. When employees stop hiding, lashing out, and lying, they impact the culture as a whole.

Subordinates can also improve their workplace environments by encouraging compassion for those at the top. It's easy to blame those in power for being mean, indifferent, and unhelpful, but it isn't very useful. It is far more productive to try to understand the mind-set of those at the top, especially the shame spirals that might be driving their behavior. Of course, the biggest trigger of any shame spiral is failure, and employees can help prevent a superior from getting sucked into a spiral of shame by doing everything they can to make sure the company (or the division, or the branch, or the department) succeeds.

Together, employees and managers can transform a culture of shame and self-consciousness into a culture of constant success. They can push themselves to tell the truth, even when it's uncomfortable. They can catch themselves lashing out in defensiveness (and apologize for it if necessary). They can practice boldness by making public presentations, or by asking for more money, or by saying no, or by setting goals, or by admitting ignorance. When everyone works together to transform shame spirals into achievement spirals, the result is almost always extraordinary.

* * *

Questions to Ask Yourself

Who could you get to know better at your company or
   even introduce yourself to?

What help do you need that you aren't asking for?

What would be the advantages of saying no when you
   mean no (instead of making a promise you don't
   have any intention of keeping)?

To what extent do you help create an atmosphere of
   openness and comfort at work? To what extent do
   you contribute to a climate of anxiety and pretense?

* * *

EN-COURAGING YOURSELF

In Washington, feeling shame just means it's time for a new career.

— BERNARD KALB

Throughout this book, we've been looking at the possibility of transforming spirals of shame into spirals of accomplishment, pride, and self-expression. We have looked at how our shame spirals trap us at work, in our relationships, and with our families. We've also looked at the importance of deconstructing our beliefs about what is embarrassing, the importance of getting the facts, and the importance of taking courageous action. We've looked at how our image-control strategies are self-defeating and counterproductive. Hopefully, by now, you're excited by the possibility of being courageous in the face of potential embarrassment. Hopefully you see an opportunity to make a clear request for something that you've been yearning for or you see new value in taking a stand for what you really believe. Hopefully you're eager to practice the art and science of Self En-Couragement.

Now, you may be asking yourself a question: How can I be courageous when all I really feel is fear? Below is an array of techniques you can use to revitalize your sense of courage when you seem to be getting in your own way. Some of these techniques will come naturally, but at first most will probably feel strange. We're not accustomed to managing our lives to accommodate both fear and determination. We usually succumb to fear or try to bulldoze our way through life as if our fears were irrelevant. The following suggestions require a shift in perspective, but they are based on well-tested psychotherapeutic and social-scientific principles.

1. TRAIN YOURSELF TO RECOGNIZE RED THOUGHTS AND TRANSFORM THEM INTO GREEN ONES. Red thoughts are those that stop us from taking a risk: "If I ask for it, he'll only say no." "If I go to the party, I'd have to tell people he dumped me." "If I call a second time, she'll think I'm a loser." Red thoughts have the ability to stop us in our tracks. We tend to listen to our red thoughts as if they were infallible. Notice how you react when someone suggests you do something you've already decided would be a bad idea. If you're like most people, you get physically tense. You may say something like "I would but I *know* what's he's like" or "*I know* how it would go" or "*I know* the way I am." See if you can hear your own capitulation to your red perspective.

Keep in mind the wise words of Walter Lippman: "For it is clear enough that under certain conditions men respond as powerfully to fictions as they do to realities, and that in many cases they help to create the very fictions to which they respond."[1]

Developing the skills of social courage means liberating yourself from the shackles of red thoughts by challenging their accuracy. As you challenge your own viewpoint, you start to see situations from a broader perspective. You begin to see that maybe you *could* do it. The operative word here is *maybe:* "Maybe I have nothing to lose." "Maybe I would blow him away with my boldness." "Maybe I would get the raise simply by demonstrating my bravery." These are yellow thoughts.

After yellow thoughts come green ones. Green thoughts propel us into action: "I'll give it a try." "I'll call until I get through." "I'll make it happen." Green thoughts are "go" thoughts. They reflect a spirit of commitment and courage.

You can think of red as stop, yellow as get ready, and green as go.

One mistake people make is blaming themselves for having red thoughts, yet we all have them. We've all taken risks in the past and promised ourselves never to do so again in the future. Instead of blaming yourself, give yourself the freedom to have red thoughts without succumbing to them. You might want to make a list of all the "rules" you have in life. The list might sound like "Never make the first move," "Never mention my fear of intimacy," "Never be the first to speak at a meeting" . . . When you get a substantial number of such rules down on paper, see if you can challenge each one. "Maybe making the first move is necessary sometimes," "Maybe mentioning my fear of intimacy would create intimacy," "Maybe by speaking first I could set the tone of the whole meeting."

Using the red, yellow, green perspective, you can take control of your own thought processes. You can take an active role in moving from self-consciousness to courage.

2. **CONCENTRATE ON THE PHYSICAL SYMPTOMS OF FEAR (USING YOUR RIGHT BRAIN).** Becoming aware of your own bodily reactions is a valuable technique for interrupting the spiral of shame. Both the fear of embarrassment and embarrassment itself are, on one level, physiological phenomena. For

the most part, however, you and I live our daily lives almost entirely unaware of changes in our physiology (heartbeat, temperature, breathing, facial tension, etc.). The more aware you become of your physiological responses, the less meaningful those responses will seem to be. The next time you have "butterflies" in your stomach, for instance, concentrate on the exact experience as you're having it. "Butterflies" is a generalization that masks the actual experience. Ask yourself questions that are as specific as possible (even if they seem silly). Do you feel something below your belly button or above? To the right or to the left?

Experiencing your physiological processes as they occur in real time will cause a mental shift. Mostly, we interpret our experiences in a left-brain manner. The left brain uses well-worn categories and classifications to make sense of reality. The left brain is like a labeling machine with a limited number of settings.

The right brain processes information in a manner that is very different from that of the left brain. Instead of relying on familiar labels, the right brain experiences life moment by moment. Artists have found that they can "see" better and draw better by processing visual information in a right-brain mode that doesn't force the messy facts of life into predictable categories.

Your left brain will resist the practice of experiencing your physiological processes as they occur in real time. Your left brain prefers generalizations like "I'm scared," "I don't want to," "I think it's stupid," "I feel sick." These generalizations will actually keep the problem you're dealing with from going away.

As you concentrate on the specific sensations of your body

as you experience them, your right brain will take over, and your left brain will "go to sleep," so to speak. When that happens, the voice in your head—the one saying things like "I'm scared," "I can't," "I don't want to," "I feel awful"—will quiet down. You will experience a kind of tranquillity. From that peaceful place, you will find yourself able to take action you wouldn't normally take.

3. "FORCE" YOURSELF TO BE AFRAID. Take advantage of famed psychologist Victor Frankl's remarkable approach to treating anxiety, paradoxical intention (PI). Frankl found that when people *try* to make something happen through sheer will, they usually fail.

You can use the technique of paradoxical intention by trying to will yourself into fear. Try to make your throat go dry. Try to clench your stomach. Try to make yourself sweat. Try to make your cheeks blush. Try to make your vision blur. Try to feel ashamed. It's virtually impossible to do.

The moment you start to feel embarrassed is the moment to practice PI. If you have to call someone to apologize for something, practice PI before you pick up the phone. Concentrate on trying to feel sheepish. Pick up the phone as slowly as you possibly can. Take five long minutes to dial the number. Make your heart beat as loudly as possible while you wait for the other person to answer.

Paradoxical intention may seem silly, but it works. Try telling someone "I've decided to be emotionally invulnerable. I'm no longer going to share with you any of my feelings or fears. I'm going to pretend to be confident and clever." Then see how long your emotional invulnerability really lasts.

4. SEEK OUT ALLIES. CREATE A COMMUNITY OF SUPPORT.
Taking risks is always easier when you have people rooting for
you, people you know are on your side. There is safety in numbers. If you want to propose a new policy at work, get a group
of colleagues to propose it with you. If you want to quit your
job to write the great American novel, find a group of novel-
writing job quitters to give you moral support.

Social scientists have long known that people feel less anxiety in situations where they are performing in conjunction
with others than in those where they find themselves performing all alone. In the 1930s, one researcher conducted a study
involving chronic stutterers. He found that the same people
who stuttered 21 percent of the time when asked to read aloud
alone, stuttered only 1 percent of the time when asked to read
in unison with a group.[2]

The importance of having allies is made vividly clear in the
research of political scientist Michael Gross. Gross studied
the rescue of Jews in France and Holland during the Nazi era,
focusing on an area of southern France where Protestants rescued nearly 2,500 Jewish refugees and a city in Holland where
Dutch Calvinists rescued some 250 Jews. Gross discovered
that those who were courageous and resisted the Nazis did so,
in large part, because they knew they were not alone in their
convictions. He concluded that courageous people get suste-
nance from their connections to other courageous people.
Without such connections, individuals are less likely to act,
though they may have all the good intentions in the world.
"Deprived of the necessary moral community," writes Gross,
"enlightened reasoners are often long on moral indignation but
short on political action."[3]

Anyone who experiences a barrier to success in society because of a condition or characteristic over which they have no control may be embarrassed by that condition or characteristic, in which case it helps to find community. Being able to identify with a larger group of people makes it easier to deal with—and to tell truth about—a particular characteristic. Originally, Raquel Welch played down her Hispanic origins because she thought they would limit her chances of success as an actress. With the growth of the Latino pride movement, many more people have "come out" as Hispanic. Today, Welch is very public about being Latina, and she has even managed to use her ethnic heritage to propel her career forward. Young gay men and lesbians tend to seek out fellow gays and lesbians as allies before coming out to their family members and friends. That way, if things don't go well, they will have people to talk to and get comfort from.

Seeking out allies is a highly pragmatic means of empowering yourself to take risks. You may have to think beyond your immediate circle of friends and family members. In fact, you may have to reach out to people you normally wouldn't choose to associate with, people you find intimidating or unfriendly or overly upbeat. Sometimes the people we tend to avoid are the ones who have the most to offer us when we're trying to expand ourselves in new ways. Consider asking someone to serve as a mentor. The more people you have lined up rooting for your success, the easier you will find it to push yourself beyond your comfort zone.

5. **GET THE KIND OF SUPPORT YOU WANT.** One of the things that we instinctively do when we're afraid of being embarrassed

is talk about our anxieties with our friends. "I'm so nervous" is something you've probably said to someone before a job interview or an athletic event or a public presentation. Communicating anxiety is effective up to a point. Unfortunately, most people don't know what to say in response, other than some version of "don't worry; you'll do great." Being told not to worry can be reassuring, but it can also be extremely irritating.

To resolve this dilemma, you need to figure out what you really want to hear from your friends. Do you want them to share their own stories of succeeding in the face of fear? Do you want advice? Do you just want someone to listen to you without saying anything in response other than "I hear you"? When you figure out what you want, then you can ask for it. "Listen, I'm really nervous about this speech I have today. I don't want any advice; I just want to hear about a time you were nervous, but you did really great anyway." Or "I have this speech to give today, and I'm really nervous. Could you give me some pointers from your experience?" Unless you ask for exactly what you want, don't be surprised if you get something else.

If being courageous is something very new for you, it may be jarring for the people in your life. They may not know how to provide the kind of support you need or want. You are going to have to train them to treat you as someone dedicated to being brave, especially if you have spent years training them to treat you as someone who "doesn't have what it takes" to tackle difficult encounters.

6. COUNT THE COSTS OF IMAGE CONTROL. Succumbing to self-consciousness has heavy costs, but we often forget or deny those costs. One way to get yourself into action is by doing

some ruthless accounting. What price are you paying for living in fear? What's the emotional toll of relying on image-control tactics to maintain face? What are the costs to your pride, your sense of freedom, your experience of being known? And what are the opportunity costs? Who aren't you meeting? What opportunities aren't you finding out about?

If you know you're having trouble taking a risk, force yourself to confront the costs of playing it safe. If you really face the facts, you'll find yourself automatically getting into action.

7. **CHOOSE ROLE MODELS WHO INSPIRE YOU.** There has been a lot of talk in the media in recent years about the importance of role models for kids. The truth is, as adults we need role models too; we just don't like to admit it.

A role model is someone who demonstrates the kind of qualities you'd like to have yourself. When it comes to being courageous, you need a role model who exemplifies social bravery. Personally, I'm inspired by all sorts of people: "won't-take-no-for-an-answer" social activists, can-do capitalists, "go-ahead-and-laugh-at-me" leaders. I like people who have equal parts sense of humor about themselves and fierce determination to succeed.

When you find a role model, study up on him or her. Read biographies, memoirs, and other pertinent books. Figure out what it is you find inspiring about that person. If the person is still alive, write him or her a letter. Try to arrange a meeting. What have you got to lose? Whether your role models are living or dead, you can start talking them up to other people. Share your excitement about the actions they took or what they accomplished. (My friend Admir's role models are George

Soros and Mother Teresa. He is always reading and talking about them. His enthusiasm is infectious.)

Edmund Morris is a writer who eagerly embraces controversy. He took an innovative approach to writing *Dutch,* a biography of Ronald Reagan, knowing in advance that his approach would be denounced by academics, on the one hand, and loyal Republicans on the other. Morris says that when he starts to lose his self-confidence before doing a courageous act, he reminds himself of the great musicians, artists, and writers who have braved public opprobrium in order to be true to their vision: "I think of Beethoven and Mozart, the Impressionists, James Joyce." He uses them as role models to inspire him to take risks.

Keep in mind that no human being is perfect. If your role model turns out to have flaws, don't get discouraged. Just keep note of any weaknesses you have in common and ways you could conquer them. Be wary of the temptation to get more interested in other people's failures than in their successes. It's no coincidence that shows about fallen stars are so popular; we all take comfort in the misfortune of others. But when it comes to getting inspired, you need to rise above the desire for gossip.

If you are true to yourself and your dreams, you may end up eclipsing your own role model. That's not a problem; just choose someone else who inspires you. Perhaps Rosa Parks. Or the president of a major company. It doesn't matter who you choose, as long as that person reminds you to strive for your best.

8. **RENT INSPIRING MOVIES.** Finding a role model is a long-term strategy; renting an inspiring movie is a short-term plan,

a quick investment in your own courage. If you are contemplating a big move, but you're stopped by self-consciousness, rent a film you know will push you down the road you really want to take. When my father wants to boost his resolve, he rents Westerns. He loves the good-guy/bad-guy simplicity and the take-action philosophy. (Personally, I'm more partial to *Star Wars,* but that too is a Western in its own way.)

If your goal is getting geared up for action, stay clear of sardonic films that are too smart for their own good. Pick blockbusters, the kind that you know will make you laugh and cry. Sometimes it's a good idea to stop the movie halfway through and take action the moment you feel inspired. Hollywood endings can be so cathartic they drain us of all resolve.

If you like the silver-screen approach to building courage, indulge your passion. Keep a list of your favorites. Buy a CD or two so you can listen to an inspiring soundtrack on your way to work. Hang posters in your cubicle or at home. Allow yourself to be the swashbuckling hero that you are.

If watching movies doesn't do it for you, try going to a play or a musical or a sports event—something, anything that will remind you of the importance of living life to the fullest. Literary critic Wayne Koestenbaum finds inspiration at the opera: "Opera has the power to warn you that you have wasted your life. You haven't acted on your desires. You've suffered a stunted, vicarious existence. You've silenced your passions. The volume, height, depth, lushness, and excess of operatic utterance reveal, by contrast, how small your gestures have been until now, how impoverished your physicality; you have only used a fraction of your bodily endowment and your throat is closed."[4] Koestenbaum's language may be over the top, but his point is valuable. You can use your choice of entertainment to motivate you, to push you into action.

9. **PLAY PRETEND.** If there's something you want to do but you're stopped by what you think others will think of you, it sometimes helps to play pretend. Playing pretend is especially helpful if you simply can't get past the distractions of self-consciousness. I know someone who likes to think out loud when he's walking down the street, but he doesn't want people thinking he's crazy. So he pretends to be talking on his cell phone. Pretending to talk on his cell phone gives him the freedom to talk to himself without having to worry about what anyone else is thinking.

Pretending can be helpful in many different situations. If you're insecure about going to a movie alone, you can put on dark sunglasses and pretend that you're rich and famous. If you want to find the courage to strike up a conversation in a café or a bar, you can tell yourself that you are getting material for your novel. Or you could tell yourself that you've got a terminal illness and today is your last day to be outgoing. Obviously there's a difference between playing a game with yourself and deceiving another. But there's nothing wrong with using your game as a conversation starter: "Hi, I'm trying to imagine what it would be like if I knew I only had one more day to live, and I realized I would want to say hi to you," etc., etc.

10. **FOCUS ON THE FUTURE.** When there's an action you want to take, but you know self-consciousness is getting in the way, it's essential to keep your eye on the future. We're easily distracted by the past. Think about what it is you really want to

accomplish. Imagine all the great things that might happen if you took the step you were considering. What doors might open up? What opportunities might present themselves? How might your relationships become that much more meaningful and special?

Obviously it's hard not to think about all the potential downsides of taking a risk. If you think about it, you can predict the worst possible outcomes with a fair degree of certainty, but the possible positive outcomes are almost limitless. Say hello to that person next to you on the bus, and it could change your life forever. You could get a new job. You could get a new best friend. You could end up richer and more famous than you've ever dreamed. We can never predict all the possible benefits of taking a risk.

Kids are great at focusing on the future. Every day my daughter asks if a new friend can come over to play. She doesn't have any worries about feeling embarrassed by her house or her toys or her parents. She just assumes that inviting a friend over to play would lead to more fun than not inviting over a friend. She focuses on the future because she's not burdened by the past.

We can all learn from little kids. We can dream often and dream big. We can remember to tell the truth, even if it might mean getting punished. We can say hello to strangers and dance in the aisles of the supermarket. We can play dress-up, and get dirty, and ask lots and lots of questions. Little kids don't think about the dangers of being true to themselves; they just look for ways to have fun. Of course, as adults we have responsibilities that we don't have as children, but wise children know how to have fun no matter what they're doing, whether it be learning to color or brushing their teeth or even putting away their toys.

When you focus on the future, you can overcome the fear of embarrassment in any situation. Use your dreams to pull you into action. Use your goals to triumph over your fears.

* * *

Action Steps

1. Turn red thoughts into green ones.
2. Concentrate on the physical sensations of fear.
3. "Force" yourself to be afraid.
4. Seek out allies.
5. Get the kind of support you want.
6. Remind yourself of the costs of being fearful.
7. Choose inspiring role models.
8. Rent inspiring movies.
9. Play pretend.
10. Focus on the future.

* * *

chapter 7 Family: From Guilt to Good Feelings

For many of us, our spirals of embarrassment, shame, and self-consciousness begin within our families. As children, we learn to worry about how we are viewed by our parents, our siblings, our grandparents, our uncles and aunts and cousins. Our worries never seem to go away, even as we mature into adults. To a certain degree we can't help but worry what our family members will think of us. And we can't help but engage in image control to avoid the feelings we associate with being viewed in a negative light.

There's nothing wrong with valuing what your family members think. In fact, family members tend to be a very good source of advice and information. But putting too much stock in others' opinions, even those of a family member, can readily lead to feelings of embarrassment and shame. And when these feelings arise, it can be all too tempting to engage in withdrawal, dishonesty, and hostility. Those image-control tactics result in further misreactions and misunderstandings, which quickly produce mutual resentment and frustration.

I'm pleased to say that a lot of the teenagers and twenty-somethings I've worked with and counseled in recent years seem to have relationships with their parents that are much more open than my peers and I ever had with ours. Family relationships are evolving in our society: Parents are learning how to listen and children are learning how to talk. At the same time, I still see plenty of people, young and old, who have distant, distrustful, dissocial relationships with their parents. Shame spirals have a way of infecting the best of families. The fear of disapproval, whether warranted or not, can keep us stuck in spirals of shame, dishonesty, dissatisfaction, and more shame.[1]

Fortunately, any spiral of shame can be transformed into a spiral of affinity and affection if you're willing to be responsible for your own self-consciousness and your own image-control strategizing. In the following sections, we will be addressing issues of self-consciousness specific to families.

Disappointment

No child wants to disappoint his or her parents. And no parent wants to disappoint his or her children. The internal yearning to be the perfect child or the perfect parent can make the slightest mistake a source of personal suffering. When we follow up a mistake with withdrawal,

deception, or aggression, we become even more shameful and embarrassed. This spiral often continues to grow and grow without end until
parent and child are equally frustrated and resentful.

Some people deal with the prospect of being a disappointment to
their parents by always doing what they think their parents want. This
has a way of leading to resentment, self-anger, and resignation. Others
pretend to do what they think their parents want but secretly do what
they want. People lie about their romantic partners, about their jobs,
about their studies, about whether or not they go to church. I know gay
men in their forties and fifties who still aren't out to their parents. Dishonesty, of course, can only lead to distance, fear of discovery, and an
ever greater sense of self-disrespect. Then there are those of us who
think we can escape the prospects of being a disappointment by avoiding contact and/or communication with our parents. We cut ourselves
off from our parents to "protect" ourselves from their disapproval.

Aaron has had to grapple with feeling like a failure. Not only did
Aaron refuse to go into the family business, he tried to start his own
company but failed miserably. He went heavily into debt and had to
borrow from his father to pay his bills. For several years, Aaron "dealt"
with his embarrassment by speaking to his parents as little as possible.
When they did speak, Aaron often took offense at the most minor criticism. Eventually, Aaron realized his strategy just wasn't working. He
came clean to his parents about his sense of shame and humiliation.
His father responded by telling Aaron how proud he was of him for trying to make it on his own in business. Aaron says he still has to push
himself to call his father, but that every time he does, he is glad for it.
(When he's feeling down, it is particularly hard for him to return his father's calls, but he makes a special effort.) And he still finds himself getting defensive every now and then, but he is able to catch himself and
admit—at least to himself—that he is going down the path of shame.
That allows him to get back into a spiral of intimacy and affection.

Liza is a nineteen-year-old African-American woman who is the
mother of a six-year-old boy. When Liza got pregnant at thirteen she

was so ashamed that she didn't tell her mother until she was seven months pregnant. Her mother was furious about having been lied to, which made Liza even more afraid to confide in her. Liza dropped out of high school and gave up her dreams of a career. Eventually, through the help of a nonprofit organization committed to improving the lives of African-American teenagers, Liza found the courage to confess to her mother her deep sense of shame. That conversation transformed their relationship and reignited Liza's sense of self-worth. Today, Liza is working toward a B.A. in finance at New York's City College so she can raise her son without ever going on welfare.

Shame spirals don't affect just children, they affect parents too. In fact, they play a double role in the lives of parents. First, parents often fear how their children will judge them. Second, they often fear how their neighbors and friends will judge them (based on their children). In both cases, parents try to behave in ways that they think will minimize the chances of "looking bad." Like their children, they often end up relying on image-control ploys that are usually counterproductive.

Though it's not much discussed in the psychological literature, most parents want their children to approve of them. They want their children to think of them as wise, well-informed, savvy, strong, successful. Most parents also want their children to think of them as loving, caring, and nurturing. They certainly don't want to be thought of as critical or cold. That alone can make it hard for parents to do the work of parenting. Not wanting to seem selfish or unkind, parents are tempted to just give children whatever they ask for. Not wanting to seem weak or ignorant, parents are tempted to feign confidence, to feign certainty, even to feign success. Louis says he's sure his father lies to him about money to seem more successful than he really is. Of course, no child wants a fake for a father or a phony for a mother. Children want their parents to be themselves, so that they, as children, can be themselves. But that's hard for most parents to remember.

Parents aren't just worried about being judged by their children; they're also worried about being judged by their friends, their neigh-

bors, even by total strangers. Most parents see their children as a re-
flection of them and, at the same time, want to be admired by their
peers. So when children fail or turn out to be "different" or follow an
unorthodox path or get in trouble, parents naturally get anxious about
what their friends and neighbors will think. Despite increasingly liberal attitudes in society, many parents would still rather keep a son's
homosexuality secret or dissuade their daughter from marrying a man
of a different race. It's usually not a matter of malice as much as it is of
self-consciousness.

It may not be obvious at first, but parents can be embarrassed by
mere indifference. When children don't make the effort to visit or call,
it can be very humiliating, especially if the indifference/apathy/neglect
is witnessed by others. At my grandmother's retirement home, there is
ubiquitous shame about the extent to which sons and daughters don't
come to visit. The sense of embarrassment (and rage) is almost palpa-
ble. Unfortunately, the residents rarely deal with their embarrassment
directly. Instead, they pretend that all is well. Generally they keep their
conversations with each other at a superficial, nonintimate level.

The good news is that it is entirely possible to transform our familial spirals of shame into spirals of mutual satisfaction and surprise.
What it takes is a willingness to deal with the embarrassment, shame,
and self-consciousness that is already there and to tell the truth about
the image-control strategizing we've been engaging in. Most of the time
we're not willing to tell the truth, however. Instead, we keep strategizing, we keep hoping that "someday" things will get better, without acknowledging we have a role to play in the way things are. This failure
to assume responsibility keeps us ashamed, and the spiral continues.

I am especially moved when parents make the effort to improve relationships with their children. It's never easy for a parent to display
vulnerability. Alice was going through a tough time in her career.
Though she didn't realize it at first, she was deeply ashamed and didn't
want her ten-year-old daughter to think of her as a failure and a bad
mother. When I suggested to Alice that she have an open and honest

conversation with her daughter about her embarrassment, Alice balked. "She'll think I'm crazy!" But when Alice saw how her own image-control tactics (keeping her concerns to herself, keeping conversations with her daughter superficial) were ultimately destined to drive her daughter away from her, Alice agreed to give it a go. "I sat her down in her bedroom. I was so nervous. I said, 'Lilly, there's something I have to ask you. Do you think of me as a failure?' And she said 'Sort of'! I was horrified. I said, what do you mean? She said, 'Well, you failed at your job, right? Just like I failed on my math quiz last week. Everyone's a failure sometimes. So what? You're my mom. I love you when you fail and I love you when you do great.' I was speechless. This from my ten-year-old daughter! I've never felt so proud in my whole life."

En-Couraging Yourself and Your Family

Breaking free from our familial spirals of shame takes effort or, more accurately, a Self En-Couraging approach. They won't disappear on their own. Left to their own devices, our shame spirals grow ever wider. Reversing them requires a conscientious application of will.

First, of course, it's necessary to deconstruct your own beliefs, both those about yourself and about your family members. Do you take it for granted that you are a disappointment? Do you tell yourself that you are a failure? And what do you assume about your family members? Do you assume that they are judging you? Do you assume that they are free from anxiety themselves?

Second, it's vital to get the facts. In families, this usually means paying as little attention as possible to rumor, innuendo, and gossip. If you think your father is disappointed in you because of something your sister said about what your mother said to your brother, you can be very sure you don't have all the facts. It's often helpful to get historical details. If you get fired, instead of avoiding your successful uncle at Passover, you might take the opportunity to ask him about his early career struggles. Chances are he had many downs before he had big ups. That kind of conversation can stop a spiral of shame from ruining a relationship.

Most of all, it's essential to be courageous. There's no way to turn a spiral of shame into a spiral of intimacy without taking a risk. Whether it's saying what you don't want to say or listening to what you don't want to hear, "going naked" or defrosting the facts, making a request or joining the party, saying no or apologizing or standing up for what you really believe in, there's no chance of turning a relationship around without making a courageous first move.

Ted was a student in a psychology class I taught at Marymount Manhattan College, a school with an emphasis on the performing arts. In the course of the semester, Ted realized he was ashamed of being "artsy" and felt like he would never be as successful or as manly as his older brother. I gave Ted a homework assignment: to call his brother and share with him his sense of shame and the strategies he'd used to keep his brother at a distance. Ted came back to class the next week glowing. He told us about the conversation he'd had with his brother and how his brother had confessed to being ashamed of being a "bad brother." The two talked openly and honestly with each other on the phone for the better part of an hour. It was clear from Ted's excitement that'd he turned a spiral of shame that might have grown his entire life into a spiral of brotherly affection and intimacy. A few weeks later Ted told us that he'd shared his newfound sense of freedom with his girlfriend and that it had brought the two of them closer together. That's how an upward spiral works: A positive result in one area leads to a feeling of pride in another that leads to further positive results everywhere in your life.

You can en-courage yourself by seeking out allies, people who will support you in being open, honest, and direct as well as those who take responsibility for their actions, apologize readily, and listen to everything others have to say. It may not be easy to find such allies at first, but you can train your friends to support you if you communicate your aims clearly.

Sex

For most children, lifelong shame and embarrassment really begin with sex. At four years old, you ask Daddy where babies come from, Daddy blushes and says, "Ask Mommy." Mommy gives an explanation that's more confusing than clarifying or overly technical. You realize that sex is something to be embarrassed about. Perhaps you got "caught" masturbating and Daddy impulsively said, "Don't do that." Thus begins a lifelong spiral of sexual shame, withdrawal, deception, and tension.

It's the great paradox of modern life that children only exist because of sex, but sex is supposed to be kept from children. We go to extraordinary lengths to shield children from sexual information, yet our efforts only make children all the more anxious and obsessed. Obviously children need rules and boundaries, but every rule needs to be balanced against the need for knowledge, awareness, and a life free from sexual shame.

It doesn't help that while we talk in euphemism and embarrassment about basic sexual realities, our culture is so erotically charged. Children cannot help but be mystified and intrigued by all the sultry bodies they see on television, all the representations of yearning and desire. It's not that these representations are bad or should be banned but that children have very few age-appropriate alternatives to this type of sexual information. In other areas, children can learn about the world through age-appropriate media. From television cartoons and illustrated storybooks, they learn about conflict, good and evil, history, geography, math, science, and so on. These days, there are even children's books to explain "pooping" and "farting." Children similarly need materials to help them understand, process their feelings about, and get answers to their questions regarding sex. By the time kids reach puberty, they've already been bombarded for years with sexually oriented material in popular culture.

Fortunately, there are a few books out there for young kids. Two of the best are *Where Did I Come From?* by Peter Mayle and, for early adolescents, *What's Happening to Me?* also by Mayle. These two books use simple, humorous, playful illustrations to illuminate the world of sex. Readers consistently describe the books as friendly and non-threatening. They are written from a child's, rather than an adult's, perspective. Parents can also buy a video version of *Where Did I Come From?* that presents the "facts of life" in cartoon form.

There are helpful books for parents too. I would especially recommend Sol Gordon's *Raising a Child Responsibly in a Sexually Permissive World* and Chrystal De Freitas's *Keys to Your Child's Healthy Sexuality,* Debra Haffner's *From Diapers to Dating: A Parent's Guide to Raising Sexually Healthy Children,* and Lynn Leight's *Raising Sexually Healthy Children: A Guide for Parents, Teachers, and Care-Givers.* These four books are based on the premise that children need to know that all their questions and feelings are legitimate.

Of course, if parents are trapped in their own spirals of sexual shame, kids will almost inevitably get sucked into the vortex. Parents have an obligation to their kids to work through their own sexual embarrassment and shame, so that they can avoid snarling their kids in confusion and anxiety. When children feel they can talk to their parents openly about sex, they grow up with the sense that they can talk to their parents about *anything.* That's the difference between a downward spiral of sexual shame and an upward spiral of sexual self-confidence.

* * *

Questions to Ask Yourself

How are you afraid of disappointing your parents? Do
    you feel you have already disappointed them?
How do you feel you have disappointed your children?
    How are you afraid of disappointing them further?
What strategies do you use to win approval from your
    parents, your family members, your children, your
    neighbors, etc.?
What conversations are you avoiding with the people
    who are most important to you?
Who could be an ally in your effort to be open, honest,
    and free?

* * *

chapter 8 Dating: En-Couraging Real Romance

When he was in college, Gary met a girl on the steps of the school library. She was smoking, he asked for a cigarette, they ended up chatting. The more they talked, the more he wanted to see her again. But he couldn't muster the courage to ask for her phone number. He imagined her giving him a fake number or simply saying no. When they parted, he was filled with regret. To this day he thinks about her and wonders what kind of life they could have had together. He's still ashamed of having let her get away without so much as a single date.

Dating has to be one of the most difficult rituals in modern life, made that much more so by the effects of self-consciousness. For almost everyone, the pleasures of dating are countered by the risks of humiliation. Who hasn't stopped themselves at some point or another from the simple act of saying hello?

The anxieties of contemporary dating go beyond saying hi. Questions abound. When do you ask for the other person's number? When do you make the first call? When do you reply? What do you wear? What do you order? Do you pay? When do you make the first move? Do you have sex on the first date? On the second? On the third?

These questions are answered over and over again by the advice columnists in fashion magazines. Each new issue of *Cosmo, Vogue, Glamour, Self, GQ,* and *Maxim* contains advice on dating. The magazines literally thrive on the anxiety of their readers. And they promote just the sort of image-control efforts that can lead to miscommunication, misunderstanding, and mutual bitterness. For those who want whole books packed with such advice, there are such best-sellers as *The Rules: Time-Tested Secrets for Capturing the Heart of Mr. Right,* the more indecorously titled *The Rules for Getting Laid,* and the comparatively old-fashioned *How to Make Anyone Fall in Love with You.*

It's almost impossible to avoid embarrassing, shame-inducing, even humiliating moments while dating. But it is possible to interact in a way that is enobling, one that leads to connectedness and intimacy rather than mutual distrust and anxiety. But that requires a willingness to shun default withdrawal, deception, and intimidation tactics in favor of Self En-Couragement. The potential payoff is a spiral of understanding and closeness.

Once upon a time, dating was only a significant issue for young people. But today, with the divorce rate so high and the lifespan so long, people find themselves dating at forty, fifty, and sixty. And new cultural trends have opened the traditional domain of dating to people who were normally barred from its doors, namely gay men and lesbians. As society evolves, the dynamics of dating are getting more and more complex. Interfaith and interracial dating, once unheard of, are now commonplace, but they too increase the chances of an awkward or embarrassing moment. These changes make being skilled at social courage all the more important.

Image Control

Sometimes it seems like dating is all about image control. We focus on having the "right" body, the "right" hair, the "right" clothes, the "right" scent. It can feel like a perilous balancing act. Most of us want to seem successful, but not show-offy. To seem sexy but not silly or sluttish. To seem sophisticated but not superior. No wonder it takes people so long to get ready for a date.

There's no question that dating will always involve a certain degree of image control. We are, after all, animals sizing one another up. We use our senses to determine whether or not the other person would make a good sexual and/or emotional partner. Who knows what will turn someone off? So we try to strut our stuff as best we can.

But when our fears of rejection cause us to start strategizing—to pull in, lash out, or make up stories—we're headed for trouble. The sad part is, most people are so accustomed to withdrawal, intimidation, and/or deception that any other alternative seems virtually impossible. This kind of resignation plagues contemporary dating. Ultimately, it reinforces a defeatist attitude toward relationships—the all too common "I don't want to get hurt" mentality—that leads people to avoid true intimacy altogether.

In this chapter we want to count the costs of image control. We tend to pay a significant price for our image-control efforts, but we often overlook those costs. In the following pages, we will confront those costs head-on, so that we can free ourselves from the trap of self-consciousness.

Pulling In

We tend to think that dating is about "chemistry" or "attraction" or "romance," but when all is said and done, dating is really about communication. Every relationship begins with that initial, sometimes awkward greeting; relationships are sustained by ongoing discussion of wants, feelings, needs, and so on; and if a relationship is going to develop into something more (or be ended for something else), clear, effective expression is essential.

Given how important communication is, one might think we'd all communicate openly and freely with our romantic partners and potential partners. But, of course, nothing could be farther from the truth. You see an attractive person in a restaurant or a museum—do you cruise over and say hi? Or do you think of a hundred reasons not to? You really want to go for Italian, *not* Indonesian. But do you say so? Or do you say, "Sure, I love anything?"

Most of us have gotten burned in the past from being open about our feelings. Or at least we think that's what happened. So we practice the art of *cautious living*: We avoid uncomfortable interactions, we set low goals, we conceal our emotions, and we engage in circumlocution.

1. *Avoiding uncomfortable interactions.* Saying hello to a stranger is an uncomfortable interaction. So is asking for a phone number. Or asking someone out. Most of the time we pull in. We allow opportunities to pass us by. Then we end up feeling bad about ourselves and, ultimately, bitter about being single.

These days, cruising (smiling, approaching, saying hello) isn't just for men. Women have won the prerogative to introduce themselves first. In fact, given the swirl of anxiety around sexual harassment, and the concern many men have with being considered sexist, sometimes a man simply won't make the first move, even if he's very interested. Women who are outgoing and confident are at a clear advantage over those who are waiting for the perfect man to come along and sweep them off their feet.

But that doesn't mean guys can afford to be passive. The "sensitive male" is a quaint concept, but it's inappropriate for anyone who actually wants to pick up someone else. Cruising requires assertiveness and the willingness to be rejected.

Fortunately, the Internet is making it easier to meet strangers. Dating websites make it possible to cruise in the privacy of your own home. And you can learn an astonishing amount about a person before making an introduction. But for some people, going on that first date is still a daunting prospect.

Most people rely to a certain degree on alcohol to deal with their inhibitions. Frank, an investment banker, says that having a few drinks is the only way he can pick up women without "stressing out." Nothing's wrong with a few drinks, but reliance on alcohol can lead to dependence. Bob Welch, former pitcher for the Los Angeles Dodgers, started drinking to deal with his fear of embarrassment in dating. "I was shy," he recalls. "I was scared to death of girls. But when I got drunk I could tell a girl I liked her . . . I also thought that if you didn't like a girl and she didn't like you, you could drink to cover it up. Very early on, I started running from my feelings, hiding instead of talking. I covered up my feelings by drinking." Today Welch describes himself as an alcoholic.[1]

There is something profoundly rewarding about being able to go up to another human being and say hello without a protective image-control ploy, without the benefit of alcohol. The pride that comes from being bold inspires further confidence and further boldness.

Besides being rewarding, being bold is constructive. Cruisers get more dates than noncruisers. People who readily express their thoughts and feelings (without being arrogant or rude) have richer conversations than those who don't, so their relationships progress faster and last longer.

Psychotherapist Albert Ellis discovered the advantages of boldness as a young man. At first, Ellis was very shy. He was ashamed of his shyness, which only made matters worse. Then, one day, he resolved to break free from the spiral of shame. He spent the day forcing himself to meet as many women as he possibly could. He said hello to every eligible young woman he saw. Eventually, Ellis went from being shy and introverted to a man about town.

Robert, a student at Syracuse University, describes how he used similar techniques to overcome his fears of rejection: "I would just force myself to talk to girls, no matter how scared I was. After a while it got easier to talk to them, and I became that much more confident."

2. *Aiming Low.* Tom, a public relations consultant, says that when he meets women who are very attractive he gets physically nervous. "I start stuttering, and my face turns red." Tom plays it safe by only saying hello to less attractive women. "When I hit on women who are less attractive, I feel more confident and suave. I figure that the women I want are out of my league, so I hit on ones that I'm positive will at least talk to me."

When you're dating, it's important to be clear about your goals. Not the goals you think you have, but the ones your behaviors reflect. Whether he realizes it or not, Tom's goal is to avoid rejection. That's a fine goal, as long as it's the one he really wants to have. If your goal is to meet the person of your dreams, I would suggest an approach different from Tom's.

It's strange to think of dating as an arena in which to set goals, but goal-setting can be as valuable in meeting people as in managing an organization—*as long as one doesn't take it too seriously.* I often encourage people to make a goal of going on X number of dates per week or per month. The biggest mistake people make is to see dating only as an avenue to something else: marriage, lifelong partnership, etc. When I hear someone say, "My goal is to get married," I know they're in trouble. Using dating to find a spouse is like using a worm to catch dinner: It's destined to work eventually, but it can take all the pleasure out of fishing in the present. The trick is a more Zenlike approach: It requires forgetting about the long-term goal of partnership and instead focusing on the fun of meeting someone new now.

3. *Emotional Concealment.* Few among us are as skilled at being emotionally vulnerable as we are at being emotionally protective. Somehow being open is more challenging. But it's also more productive.

Men in particular are prone to emotional concealment. Whether it's nature or nurture, the average male isn't very skilled at sharing himself. He always seems to be afraid of getting laughed at or wounded. So he hides behind the blank face of nonemotion. Alas, few women find this attractive. It's no coincidence that emotionally expressive guys (especially those with a good sense of humor) always seem to get the girls.

Russell Friedman is the executive director of the Grief Recovery Institute and coauthor of *The Grief Recovery Handbook: The Action Program for Moving Beyond Death, Divorce, and Other Losses.* When Friedman was forty-three, his second marriage came to an end. Soon after that, as often happens after a divorce, his finances took a downturn. He was suddenly headed for bankruptcy. He was utterly embarrassed. "I felt an incredible sense of failure. Like I was the stupidest man in the world. The biggest loser on the planet. Dating again was horrible. I hated dating. I didn't feel I was good at it. I never understood dating. A friend gave me a woman's number. I left this rambling message on her machine. I said, 'I feel so stupid, like a teenager who doesn't know what to say or do.'"

Though Russell was emotionally frazzled and embarrassed, his candor paid off. "The great thing was, Alice called me back and said the reason she was returning my phone call was that she was impressed by my honesty." He and Alice started dating. But Russell was still grappling with his own sense of shame. "One day I looked at her and said, 'I just don't understand why you would want to be with me. I've blown two marriages and I'm about to go bankrupt.' Then she did the sweetest thing. She just leaned forward and kissed me. Didn't say a word. She just kissed me." Russell and Alice eventually got married and have been together for fifteen years.

Breaking up with someone can be just as challenging as starting a relationship. There's the embarrassment of being single again. Breaking up with someone also raises the spectre of seeming "mean," and in our society, which places a premium on being nice, no one wants to be viewed as unkind. The moment you break up with someone you become the "bad person," and you know your erstwhile significant other and all of his or her friends are going to judge you for your gesture. Since there is almost no way to break up with someone that doesn't leave the other person feeling momentarily humiliated and hateful, you're trapped. However you do it, whatever you say, you're going to be resented, criticized, and branded as insensitive. (No matter what you say or when you say it, chances are you're going to be vilified at least for a while. Your ex will pick up the phone, call a friend, and once the tears are over, destroy your character. "He said we weren't meant for each other. What does that mean?! 'Meant for each other'?! That was the best he could come up with. He's completely out of touch with his feelings. And the best part is, he waited to do it on the day I had a really important meeting for work. He knew I had this meeting. Like he couldn't have mentioned we weren't meant for each other last week!") So instead of giving up face, we just let things drag on. In fact, we're probably all guilty of having done it: We've delayed, forestalled, put off the inevitable. Eventually it becomes a form of emotional deception.

Given the inevitable awkwardness of breaking up, speaking the words is always an act of courage. The temptation to put it off is so strong, resisting the urge to procrastinate is something that deserves acknowledgment. Your ex will get over it soon enough, and in the long run be grateful for your candor (even if he or she never says so). No one wants to be in a relationship with someone who's only there out of pity. By breaking up with someone you're not interested in, you restore that person's dignity. Someday, perhaps, we'll collectively realize that being the one who is left in a relationship always feels awful. Then people will break up with each other without the amount of drama that we currently engage in. The breaker-upper will waste no time in calling things quits, and the breakee will experience gratitude for the other's honesty. Both ex's will share their feelings of nervousness, apprehension, relief, appreciation, caring, and love. Then they will go their separate ways. The call to the best friend will sound something like "We broke up today. I was really moved by his honesty and courage. Maybe someday we'll get back together again; right now I'm just excited to see who else is out there."

4. *Circumlocution*. All too often we communicate, but we do so so poorly or in such a roundabout fashion or we omit so many important details that our communication has no impact. The following was told to me by Jason, who continued to live with his wife, Michelle, even after they were officially separated:

> Michelle and I were separated for a year and planning to get divorced, but I moved back in with her in her apartment in order for us both to save money on rent. People do things like that in New York. Some people have such great apartments, neither person ever moves out; they just put up dividers to split the space. Anyway, I was living with Michelle when I met this other girl, Kara. I was too embarrassed to tell Kara I was still living with my wife, so I kind of avoided the whole thing. I told her where I lived but made it sound like I was alone. So I'm in the apartment, and I get this phone call late at night. Of course, it's Kara, and Michelle comes out of the bathroom and sees me on the phone and calls across the room, "Who are you talking to?! Why are you giving out my number?!" Kara hears the whole thing. I didn't know what to say. Things with Kara just sort of dissolved after that.

Trumping Up the Truth

Dating and deception seem to go hand in hand. Once upon a time, women wore falsies to make their breasts look bigger and men wore toupees to make their hair seem thicker. Fortunately we're past all that (now that we have implants and Rogaine), but the white lying continues.

Andy once went on a date with a woman he was very interested in. Andy has a perspiration problem: When he's nervous, he sweats. At dinner, he was so nervous, the sweat was trickling down his face. He kept excusing himself to go the bathroom, pretending he was getting important calls on his cell phone. Finally he gave up the ruse and de-frosted the facts: "I have to level with you," he told his good-looking dinner partner. "I'm petrified because this is the first date I've been on in a really long time that matters to me." The woman smiled. "It's okay, I'm nervous too." Andy was immediately relieved. The sweating stopped. They had a terrific time together, and Andy felt proud of himself for being honest.

Sometimes we can't bring ourselves to tell the truth because we're just too ashamed of what we feel. Barbara, an actress now in her late forties, tells the following story:

When I was twenty-two, I was engaged to a light-skinned black man with this sexy British accent. I was head over heels in love. Right before he had to go abroad to finish college he introduced me to his family. He told me that they would take care of me until he returned. I was shocked when I saw that they were really dark skinned. I panicked. I was afraid of being connected to a very dark-skinned family. What would people say? Looking back I'm ashamed of how I reacted, but at the time I was a mess. I broke off the engagement a month after he left. I never told him the real reason because I knew I wasn't supposed to be prejudiced, and on top of that I didn't want to hurt his feelings. I didn't want to make him self-conscious about being black.

A less drastic case is illustrated by Steve. Steve went to drinks, dinner, and a movie with a younger man who never once offered to pick up the tab. After the movie, the younger guy said, "Let's get dessert." Steve wanted to explain his real reasons for declining but instead just said he was tired and wanted to go to sleep early.

Whether or not deception is morally wrong is beside the point. The more we lie—or withhold important facts—the more mentally and physically tired we become. Over time we lose our vitality. We end up walking around with a heavy collection of undelivered sentiments, observations, and opinions.

For gay men, the closet is almost certain to create tension. Gay dating always gets complicated when one person is "more out" than the other. If a man is only out to a few friends while his date is out to everyone, the former will probably spend a lot of time worrying about who's saying what to whom. Since dating is a public affair, it's very hard to control the flow of information. That kind of anxiety can strain relationships quickly. Kip describes what it was like to date a man in the closet: "It felt degrading that he was always trying to pretend I was just his 'roommate.' He didn't want me to have a painting on the wall because it had a naked man in it. I said, 'Hello, the painting on the other wall has a naked woman in it.' But he didn't care. He didn't want me to answer the phone when certain people called. He even censored the books on the bookshelf."

Lashing Out

Intimidation is a less common—or at least less commonly recognized—image-control strategy in dating. Nonetheless, when embarrassment is a factor, intimidation often follows suit.

Most of the time when we lash out, we do so with a strong sense of self-justification: "He didn't call me all day!" "She let me pay for dinner, and I didn't get anything in return!" "He spent the entire evening looking at other women!" When we're feeling humiliated, it's natural to want to strike back. The more humiliated we feel, the more righteous we become. At some point or another you've probably said something like "I'm not calling him/her. Let him/her call me first." Or you've arrived late to show you cannot be taken for granted. Or you've spent an evening making a show of your suffering.

Sometimes dating makes us act like teenagers. Or little children. Richard admits that the first time he went on a date with June, he was embarrassed because his car wasn't as nice as her father's. When June made a joke about it, Richard felt humiliated. From then on, he took every opportunity he could find to make a dig about June's father. They continued to date and eventually got married, but the tension never ended. Richard felt like he would never be good enough for June. Eventually, they divorced.

These are examples of lashing out in response to embarrassment. But sometimes we lash out to prevent embarrassment before it happens. Brian, a newspaper reporter and Ivy League graduate, is an example. Having suffered plenty of rejection in his day, he's developed a cynical approach to picking up women. He'll compliment a woman on her smarts and then make a dig about her looks. He figures piercing a woman's self-esteem will make her hungry for more positive attention. (The anxieties of dating have a way of making people forget about their sense of right and wrong.) I watched Brian in action, and while his approach did seem to work, it also created more emotional distance between him and his prey. His intimidational strategy was hardly a practical way to inaugurate a long-term relationship.

Sarcasm is another form of lashing out. It's a way of protecting against mockery. If I make fun of you first, you can't make fun of me. Some people find they cannot shut off their sarcastic sense of humor.

They make cutting remarks even when they would rather be gentle or considerate. I've found that sarcasm is often a shield to protect an easily wounded heart.

One of the most ubiquitous forms of intimidation, especially among urban gay men, is "attitude." The elements of attitude include affecting boredom, avoiding eye contact with lesser mortals, and finding fault with anything and everything. Attitude is such a prevalent phenomenon in the gay male world that many men won't go out to bars or clubs because they so dislike the feeling of being summarily dismissed. Even those who are very good-looking can find the gay world oppressive. "The self-questioning is constant," says Rob, a handsome gay man. "Am I cute enough? Are my abs tight enough? Am I young enough? Am I wearing the right thing? Day after day, night after night. It's horrible." Of course, attitude exists in the straight world too. Anyone who is high status (in looks, wealth, or "popularity") and has reason to fear losing that status is likely to display attitude. Attitude is a means of keeping away (or, one could say, keeping down) those of lesser status. But superciliousness invariably leads to a sense of loneliness. The more we set ourselves above others, the less connected we feel and, ultimately, the more dead we become inside. It's no wonder that among the most attractive, most successful, most haughty gay men, drug abuse is such a serious problem. Attitude leads to alienation, which leads to a craving for connection, often sought, unsuccessfully, by taking drugs like Ecstasy and crystal meth.

Spirals

The reliance upon image-control strategies in dating can easily lead to miscommunication and misunderstanding. The pitfalls of withdrawal and intimidation are cleverly illustrated in a scene in the one-hundredth episode of *Friends*. Monica and Chandler are "casually" dating; both want more, but neither wants to be the first to say so. They are also both eager to keep their relationship a secret from their mutual friends. In a sitcom twist of events, Monica agrees to go on a double date with Rachel and two hunky male nurses. When Chandler finds out he gets upset, of course, but he tries to play down his sense of wounded pride. Instead of telling Monica how he really feels he pretends as if nothing's wrong. His withdrawal causes her to lash out.

> *Chandler* [spotting Monica]: Oh-hey-hey-hey! There you are!
>
> *Monica:*   Umm, listen there's something I think you should know.
>
> *Chandler:*   Oh, is this about you—you dating the nurse? Yeah, Joey already told me, and I am so, so fine. I mean, you and I we're just, y'know, we're nothing, we're goofin' around. [Withdrawal]
>
> *Monica:*   Umm, actually I was about to tell you that I was, I was going to get out of it, but hey, if we're just 'goofing around' then uh, maybe I *will* go out with him. [Lashing out]
>
> *Chandler:*   Fine! Maybe I will too!

Chandler says that he and Monica are just "goofin' around," but what he doesn't realize is that she actually wants him to express his passion for her. She interprets his laid-back attitude as rejection. Insulted, she lashes out. Chandler, in turn, lashes back. If this were a real-life scenario, chances are good that Chandler and Monica would be finished.

I would venture to guess that 80 to 90 percent of all relationships that end do so because of some version of this shame spiral. Partners hide their true feelings; they withdraw or lie or lash out. Mutual, genuine communication becomes impossible. Dissolving the relationship before it gets too serious seems like the only logical answer.

Sex is obviously one of the most embarrassment-inducing aspects of dating. Everything from trying to unhook a bra to discussing contraception can make "romantic" moments awkward.

We learn to be embarrassed about sex from our parents, our teachers, our peers. I have met very few adults who are entirely comfortable talking about their sexual proclivities: their wants, their needs, their desires. On the other hand, I have met quite a few people who are embarrassed by their own embarrassment around sex. We live in such a sex-saturated culture that it is easy to think everyone else is more sexually sophisticated than you are.

Like other sources of embarrassment, sexual awkwardness usually results in misreactive image control. You want to ask your partner to use a condom, but you feel too awkward about it, so you say nothing. Your partner asks you if you're enjoying yourself; you aren't, but you lie. Your partner makes a joke about your sexual history; you get defensive and lash out. These types of misreactions only make real intimacy that much more difficult.

All too often we deal with our sexual embarrassment by drinking or taking drugs, which increases the likelihood of making a very bad spur-of-the-moment decision to have unsafe sex. Alcohol, marijuana, cocaine, Ecstasy, and other drugs impair our ability to think carefully and make wise choices.

Our sexual shame spirals are almost invariably fueled by our beliefs about masculinity and femininity. The guy who thinks he's macho by not using a condom, the girl who thinks she's sexier when she's drunk, are trapped in gendered image-control schemes. Beliefs about what's masculine and what's feminine readily constrain our ability to communicate our sexual fantasies, wants, and needs. Many women have a hard time asking for oral sex. Many straight guys are embarrassed because they like having their nipples played with. We would all benefit by becoming more aware of how gender beliefs underlie—and undermine—our sexual interactions.

Pornography, erotic magazines, and romance novels can be both liberating and further shame inducing. On the one hand, erotic materials can help couples break through their sexual barriers; on the other hand, the buff and waxed stars of hard-core cinema can easily trigger feelings of low self-esteem. The idealized imagery in romance novels can likewise promote feelings of inadequacy.

(One surefire way to transform a spiral of sexual shame into a spiral of sexual freedom is to spend time on a nude beach. Nude beaches are dramatically democratic: They vividly demonstrate that people come in all shapes and sizes. I would encourage anyone who's never been to a nude beach to visit one. The mere act of taking one's clothes off on a sun-drenched beach in the company of other equally naked folks can do wonders for one's sense of self-confidence in the bedroom.)

As long as our culture continues to treat sex as something secretive and ultrasignificant, it will continue to be a source of embarrassment and shame. But those feelings of self-consciousness can be reduced through communication. It's no coincidence that the word *intercourse* refers both to the sex act and to the act of communicating through speech. Intercourse is a form of connection, and the more we communicate our sexual thoughts and feelings openly, the more fully we are able to connect on every level.

Dating: Being Courageous in a Crunch

A Self En-Couraging approach to dating requires three critical steps: (1) deconstructing your assumptions, (2) getting the facts, and (3) taking intelligent risks.

When it comes to our personal relationships, we tend to put great stock in our "gut feelings," our first impressions, and our firm beliefs. Even when we think we're being extremely rational, we're usually anything but. It's like we think we know all there is to know about ourselves and others and dating. People often begin statements with "I know myself, and I need . . ." or "I know men and they . . ." or "I know women and they . . ." We speak in platitudes: "On a first date, you should never . . ." "On a first date you should always . . ." All too often, our platitudes get in the way of our relationships.

Our platitudes about sex are some of the most obviously uninformed: "If I do X, he won't respect me." "If I ask her to do Y, she'll think I don't love her." We take it for granted that our fantasies are embarrassing, our past activities shameful.

Self En-Couragement in dating begins with deconstructing such platitudes. It isn't hard to do. For one thing, you and I are constantly growing and changing; we are in a continuous state of becoming. So our beliefs about ourselves are always already outdated. The idea that one has an immutable personality formed by nature and nurture is a holdover from late-nineteenth-century notions of psychological development. Our personalities are constantly evolving as a result of the interactional moves we make. Each time we speak, each time we act, we redefine ourselves in relationship to others. Consequently, we redesign the future.

Deconstructing the truth also means questioning our assumptions about human motivation. All too often we assume that we know why someone else is doing what he or she is doing. Instead of going to the trouble to try to empathize, we jump to conclusions. He didn't call because he's not interested. She didn't smile because she thinks I'm a jerk. The problem is we choose friends who will agree with us about our interpretations, even when they are facile.

As we let go of our assumptions and beliefs, we naturally become more interested in the facts. What really happened: when, where, why, and how? A Self En-Couraging approach to dating is based on a scientific mind-set. It means getting all the data before making a conclusion. It means asking questions you wouldn't normally ask and waiving the right to make assessments you would normally be inclined to make.

Deconstructing your assumptions and getting the facts allows you to take risks intelligently. Taking intelligent risks includes everything from voicing your private thoughts to making clear requests to "going naked" to defrosting the facts. The more courageous you are in dating, the more you will be able to turn your spirals of self-consciousness into spirals of success.

The following story illustrates how even the worst experience can be turned into a successful one. The story is uncomfortably graphic— it has to do with a woman getting sudden diarrhea on a date—but I've included it because it is so vivid as a demonstration of the value of social courage. Tina is a woman who once went on a bike-riding date with a Brazilian man to the Crown Heights section of Brooklyn, where they ate lots of rich, spicy foods. Then they started biking back to Manhattan. Along the way, Tina could tell she was going to get the runs, but she thought she could make it home. When they got to Prospect Park, she realized she wasn't going to make it. She jumped off her bike and ran behind a tree. But it was too late. Before she could even lower her Spandex biking shorts, she lost control of her bowels. Hiding behind a tree, she started to cry and searched for leaves to clean herself with. "Do you need help?" her date called from afar. "NO! GO AWAY!" she yelled through her tears. Then to make matters worse, she saw two young men headed down the path in her direction. She pulled up her shorts and ran to her bike. She recalls: "I was just going to get away as fast as I could. But my date said, 'Wait, it's okay; I've got rags and water in my backpack.'" In the space of a moment, Tina made a fateful decision. She decided not to give in to her feelings of shame and embarrassment. Still crying, she turned around and accepted his offer of help. He took her hand and walked her to a secluded fountain. There he kept her laughing while she cleaned up. Then they went back to his apartment, where she took a shower, and they spent the evening together. "I've never felt so taken care of by someone. He saw me at my most pathetic, my most vulnerable, and yet he still wanted to be with me. Normally I would have just biked away and never returned his phone calls. Instead I let him take care of me. It sounds weird, but it turned out to be one of the most romantic experiences of my life. And I grew from it. That's the most important thing. I realized I could let someone care for me. I didn't have to be strong or perfect or pretty. I could be completely helpless and human. I can't tell you the kind of difference that's made in my relationships with men. I don't have anything to hide anymore. It's like I can trust people with my deepest secrets."

Success in dating often comes down to counting the costs of image control. All too often, we overlook the costs of our image-control strategies. But those costs are often numerous and great. When we stop trying to "look good," when we stop trying to "protect" ourselves, real self-confidence and thus real romance become possible. When we trust others, we turn our spirals of shame into spirals of connection.

* * *

Questions to Ask Yourself

How do you aim low in the dating arena?

What ways do you use to hide what you're really feeling when you're on a date?

When do you get dishonest?

When do you lash out?

What steps could you take to be more courageous when dating?

* * *

chapter 9 Relationships: Resparking the Spiral of Intimacy

Introduction

In the last chapter we looked at our spirals of self-consciousness in dating. But shame spirals can also significantly affect our long-term relationships. Often we're afraid to admit things we've done or said. Or we're too embarrassed to admit how we really feel or what we really want. Intent on keeping up a good image, we keep our partners at a distance. Our relationships stay at a superficial level. We strive to protect ourselves from getting hurt, instead of allowing ourselves to be vulnerable for the good of the relationship.

When it comes to sex, a certain degree of shame and embarrassment seems almost inevitable. Who isn't ashamed of sexual experiences they've had (or haven't had)? Who isn't embarrassed to admit his or her fears and fantasies?

But sex isn't the only subject that's hard to talk about. Money is equally troublesome. Many, if not most, couples find it hard to be open and honest when it comes to finances. It's just so easy to feel ashamed of having lost money or of having too much money or of not saving money or of being stingy with money or of spending it lavishly or of not investing it wisely.

Drug use, alcoholism, psychological problems, and religious differences can all be sources of embarrassment and self-consciousness in a marriage or partnership. Sometimes couples will ignore an embarrassing issue, pretending that it doesn't exist. Other couples will argue heatedly any time an embarrassing issue is raised.

Up until now, we've looked primarily at personal image-control strategies and personal spirals of shame. But when you look at relationships, you have to pay attention to costrategies and cospirals. Costrategies can mean mutual pulling in or mutual lashing out. Sometimes a costrategy can involve an endless spiral of deception and denial. Partners all too often send signals to each other about what they are uninterested in hearing. It can take real courage to contradict those signals for the sake of the integrity of the relationship.

The more shame and embarrassment infect our relationships, the more we have a tendency to withdraw into silence, to lash out, to fail to ask for what we really want, to say yes when we mean no, to lie, to conceal our true feelings. And alas, instead of going away with time, shame and embarrassment seem to grow stronger the longer they go unaddressed. As I hope this chapter shows, the quality of our relationships is directly related to our ability to acknowledge shame and embarrassment when they arise and to recognize when our actions are driven by our fears.

Keeping the Lights Off

Say "shame" and the first word that usually comes to mind is *sex*. Sex has been wrapped in shame for at least two thousand years and maybe more. Of course, one of the very first stories of the Bible—Eve and the serpent—is about the origins of sexual shame. The Old Testament stresses that the sexual parts of the body are inherently unclean. Traditional Jews, Christians, and Muslims are supposed to eschew an interest in anything erotic that doesn't lead directly to reproduction by a husband and his wife.

On a social and cultural level, we've come a long way vis-à-vis sex. Topics that were once completely taboo are now discussed on morning talk shows. Television dramas, especially those on cable, deal directly with the realities of premarital sex, homosexuality, birth control, abortion, and so on. Still almost everyone experiences a certain degree of sexual embarrassment or shame at some point or another. Premature ejaculation, impotence, and inorgasmia are problems that virtually all couples must deal with eventually. Regardless of how common these problems may be, they almost invariably give rise to embarrassment. Even the most sexually sophisticated couples generally find it difficult to talk about such issues openly.

Sex can be complicated by embarrassment even when no real problems are present. Since most Americans are dissatisfied with their bodies, sex often involves near-constant anxiety. Some people keep the lights off, others suck in their gut, others try never to take off all their clothes. The standards set by Hollywood movies, advertising, and hardcore pornography can make any physical imperfection seem shameful. That's why women are now having their belly buttons reconstructed, their breasts made bigger, their vaginas redesigned. It's why men are getting implants in their chests, their arms, their calves, and their penises. Even after sex, couples must contend with the nakedness issue. Individuals uncomfortable with their bodies may quickly find themselves embarrassed in front of their partners.

For new couples, the fear of sexual fumbling is a given. Potential bedroom faux pas include everything from inadvertently passing gas to requesting oral sex at the wrong time to glancing at one's watch. And when someone does do the "wrong" thing, he or she will probably rely on the usual strategies of image control—withdrawing, lying, or lashing out—strategies that can make the situation that much worse.

In the bedroom a man must steer carefully between the Scylla of temporary impotence and the Charibdys of premature ejaculation. Men don't have the option of "faking it." And the more nervous a man is, the more likely he will find his body working against him. So, for men, embarrassment is a very real issue.

Women, of course, have their own concerns: from looking pretty to smelling sweet. Girls and women receive so many cultural messages about what they should and shouldn't feel in the bedroom that it's almost impossible for them not to become anxious about their bodies. Rare is the woman who doesn't at some point pull in or lash out or lie or conceal what she's really feeling.

Masturbation is an especially discomforting issue for many couples. Even today, several decades after the sexual revolution of the 1960s and '70s, many women and some men are easily embarrassed about their autoerotic activities. Culturally, masturbation is still closely associated with weakness and self-indulgence. Despite the discussion of the subject on shows like *Seinfeld* and *Sex and the City,* masturbation still feels shameful to many people. Women are often loath to admit to doing something so "dirty" as touching themselves. People are even—or should I say especially—embarrassed by the masturbatory practices of their partners. Discovering that one's partner occasionally enjoys some "private time" can be very threatening. Since many people internalize the belief that relationships can be judged by the degree of mutual gratification in the bedroom, a partner's masturbatory activities can seem to undermine the very legitimacy of the relationship. "What would my mother think if she knew?" is a question that may fly through a woman's mind (since daughters often learn from their mothers that it's the woman's job to keep her husband satisfied). "What would my friends think if they knew?" is a question likely to fly through a man's (since in the sexual arena, men usually seek approval from their male peers).

Linked to the issue of masturbation is pornography. Pornography continues to have a negative association for many people (despite the vast number of people who purchase it). Whereas single people can consume pornography without anyone else's knowledge, partners in a relationship cannot often hide their pornographic interests for long. People who are determined to have their partners view them as "moral," "decent," "liberated," etc., will often go to great lengths to keep their erotic magazines and videos secret. And, just as with masturbation, one person's use of pornography can be considered embarrassing by the other. The realization that one's partner consumes pornography may inspire feelings of self-doubt and shame.

More and more, popular culture makes it clear that human beings are as diverse in their sexual fantasies as they are in their culinary preferences. And the Internet has made it easier for individuals with unusual erotic tastes to find comfort in the company of strangers. But erotic embarrassment persists. Men find it hard to tell their partners their fantasies of being dominated; women find it hard to share their enthusiasm for four-letter words. Fantasies of cross-dressing and "getting it on" with another person of the same sex probably remain the most common sources of erotic anxiety (especially for men).

Sometimes we can accept our own desires and even act on them, as long as we don't have to discuss them with our partners. An episode of *Sex and the City* comes to mind. In the show, Miranda is dating someone who likes it when she inserts her finger into his rectum during sex. One day, after their lovemaking is over, she raises the subject.

He is so embarrassed, he rolls over and refuses to talk to her. Eventually he calls off the relationship. Miranda is shocked. Her friends explain to her that there are some aspects of sex that men enjoy but have no interest in talking about. Miranda decides she will be more careful about the conversations she has with her partners in the future. She adopts a long-term strategy of calculated reticence.

While intimacy between two partners is supposed to grow over time, most couples find that sex becomes harder to talk about as a relationship matures. This is because they develop costrategies that can keep them trapped in familiar habits and patterns. Established costrategies must be abandoned if both partners are going to communicate openly about topics they've previously managed to skirt. The woman who, after twenty years of marriage, suddenly suggests switching positions risks embarrassing herself and her husband in two ways: by revealing her own dissatisfaction and by highlighting their mutual history of costrategic avoidance. The latter may be more embarrassing to the husband than the former. No one wants to admit they've spent years avoiding an important conversation, even if it's about sex.

Much more serious than the embarrassment that comes from having a desire to switch positions is the shame or embarrassment that generally surrounds having been sexually abused as a child or raped or assaulted as an adult. For anyone who has been violated sexually, merely talking about the experience can be extremely difficult. Compounded by the usual shame and embarrassment surrounding sex is a range of negative feelings, often very hard to articulate or even grasp. For one thing, we live in a culture that is suspicious of victimhood. We like to think that every person is somehow to blame for their own problems. A related issue is that we live in a culture that denigrates passivity. To admit to having been sexually violated is to admit to having been in some way passive, i.e., unable or unwilling to fend off the violator. Even for an adult, admitting to having been the passive victim of a childhood sexual exploitation can be excrutiatingly difficult because it leaves you so vulnerable. Likewise, our world celebrates winners, not losers, and admitting to having been sexually exploited is, in a way, to admit to having been a loser. For all these reasons and many others, men and women who have been sexually abused usually find it difficult to discuss their situation even with their spouses or partners.[1]

Brad Blanton, who runs workshops on honesty, says that people will carry guilty sex secrets around with them their entire lives and never confide in anyone, even their romantic partners. "I've heard it all," he says, referring to the revelations made by participants during his workshops. "The only thing that's shocking is the amount of shame that people feel. And they keep that shame locked up inside. We spend our entire lives walking around scared half to death that someone is going to find out who we screwed or what we screwed or what we wish we could have screwed."

One thing most people don't realize is the extent to which they subtly (or not so subtly) discourage their partners from being honest about sex. When one person makes it plain that infidelity is the breaking point of the relationship, the other is likely to adopt a strategy of silence. Of course, every young bride thinks her husband is the exception to the rule, but such romantic fantasies are sociologically silly. Human beings (especially males) don't seem to be particularly monogamous, so a certain amount of realism is in order. It would be nice if monogamy were the norm, or if threats of divorce were enough to keep partners from straying, but that doesn't seem to be the case. All such threats seem to do is drive the truth underground and exacerbate existing tensions and guilt.

Fortunately there's really no need for couples to stay trapped in spirals of sexual shame. With marriage counselors, sex therapists, and Viagra, couples have plenty of resources to help them eliminate embarrassment and shame from their lives. Of course, partners have to be willing to question their own assumptions about what's embarrassing, and they have to be interested in getting the facts. Many people who are embarrassed because they "never" have sex stop feeling self-conscious when they realize that they have sex more often than the national norm. Just as important as self-questioning and getting the facts is taking courageous action. It's possible to turn around any spiral of shame if you are willing to have that difficult conversation you've been putting off for years.

Ray and Ellen were so resigned about their sex life that they stopped having sex. Ray had affairs (which he didn't even bother to lie about), and Ellen contemplated divorce. Ellen knew that I had experience writing and teaching about human sexuality, so she asked me for help. For various reasons they were both disinclined to see a marriage counselor, so we arranged a three-way call. On the call, Ray said that he had stopped suggesting sex with Ellen because he was ashamed that she never wanted to have sex with him. Ellen found this shocking. "You're the one who never wants to have sex with me!" Both of them had adopted image-control tactics of withdrawal to protect themselves from feelings of embarrassment. Ellen also shared the fact that she was humiliated by Ray's extramarital encounters. At first Ray got defensive, but then he confessed to feeling guilty himself. By the end of the call we'd set up an arrangement: Ray would stop having affairs, and he and Ellen would have sex at least once a week. As we created the new arrangement, they sounded like two new human beings. They were both laughing and talking about the future with excitement.

Sex doesn't have to be different from other areas of life. It does evince greater feelings of vulnerability, but that just means that talking and listening are all the more important. The basics of turning around a spiral of sexual shame are no different from those for turning around a spiral of shame at work or with a family member: questioning your own assumptions, getting the facts, and taking courageous action. I was inspired by the way Ray and Ellen found a pragmatic approach to their marital difficulties. Once they started talking and listening to each other, all the emotional drama disappeared. The spiral of anger, hurt, and humiliation gave way to a new spiral of intimacy, joy, and, the potential for sexual satisfaction.

The Financial Factor

These days money may be a more discomforting subject than sex. Not only is the economy struggling, but money concerns are just not talked about the same way sexual concerns are. Whereas sexual issues get plenty of play in movies and on television, money matters remain comparatively taboo.[2] But for many, if not most couples, money issues bring up feelings of shame and embarrassment.

Personal debt is an issue that is of growing concern for the average American because credit-card companies are making it easier and easier to get credit. But many people feel ashamed of being in debt, and it can affect relationships. Says personal-debt expert Robin Leonard, "Most people who are having debt problems or have a lot of credit, particularly when they're in a new relationship or a new marriage where only one of them brings the debt into the relationship, are very embarrassed, very ashamed of it."[3] That shame and embarrassment can set the stage for a spiral of emotional withdrawal, embarrassment, and further withdrawal. If you have a habit of spending money to deal with your shame, that can mean even more debt and more of an emotional dilemma. Again, the three elements of a Self En-Couraging approach to excellence are vital: (1) deconstructing your own beliefs about what's embarrassing, (2) getting the facts, and (3) taking intelligent risks.

Melissa, an actress, knew that her husband, Steve, was having trouble with his chiropractic practice, but she had no idea how bad the problem really was. Realizing she needed to get the facts, she decided to examine the books. It turned out they were in serious debt: $50,000. Steve had been too ashamed to even calculate the extent of the problem. Melissa took the courageous step of insisting that she be the one to manage Steve's books. At first Steve was reluctant to turn over so much control of his business to his wife, who had no financial background, but Melissa stood her ground. After a four-hour conversation, Steve agreed to let Melissa manage his business finances. Melissa, in turn, promised to deal with their finances from a professional, non-emotional perspective.

When one person earns less money than the other, it also sets the stage for a shame spiral, especially, given the nature of gender roles in our society, if the person making less money is the man. Doug is a schoolteacher who used to be embarrassed that he earned less than his fiancée. Even though Doug wanted to buy her an engagement ring, he couldn't afford a diamond. Instead of explaining this up front, he pretended as if there were no issue to discuss and simply ignored the ring question, hoping it would somehow go away. Of course, it didn't. Fortunately, when his fiancée finally asked him what he planned to do about a ring, he fessed up to feeling like a failure as a man and a mate. She assured him that an expensive ring was unnecessary and that his sense of shame about their finances was equally needless. "I felt closer after that," says Doug. "I felt like we could really talk to each other. I got more excited about getting married. And it wasn't just the money thing. It was the idea that we could solve any issue through conversation."

One thing partners often try to hide from each other are their spending habits. Embarrassment about consumption leads easily to lying. My stepfather used to buy pieces of American folk art the way some people buy cigarettes. Every other day he would come home with a new weathervane or antique cabinet. Since there were weeks when there wasn't a penny in the bank, he was genuinely embarrassed about his spending habits and would often lie to my mother about the cost of a new acquisition.

Just as embarrassing for some people is getting ripped off. Americans pride themselves on their ability to get a good deal. We may not be accustomed to fierce negotiation in open-air markets, but we know (or are supposed to know) how to hunt for a bargain. "Never buy retail" is a value passed down in many families. So when you realize you've been ripped off on a big purchase, it may be too embarrassing to admit to anyone else, even to your partner.

One of the most embarrassing financially related events is getting fired. Americans have such a strong work ethic that to be fired is essentially to be declared a failure. For men it can be tantamount to being a bad husband. The word *fired* literally means "getting pushed away, rejected, expelled." It is no surprise that some spouses will lie about having been fired, saying that they quit or were "downsized." Others will lash out, getting snappish or sarcastic. The late Eugene Raudsepp, former president of Princeton Creative Research, a New Jersey–based consulting firm, wrote about getting fired in the *National Business Employment Weekly:* "Whatever the reason, getting fired can be one of life's most stressful experiences. The higher you are in the corporate structure, the greater the harrowing impact . . . Ashamed, [many people] avoid friends or assume friends are avoiding them. Their relationships with their immediate family also suffer as they grow defensive, cynical, and bitter. Often they reach complete despair before the self-healing process takes over and they can get back on track again."[4] The truth is, it doesn't take getting fired to feel ashamed. Losing one's job for any reason can be embarrassing. In Dominique Deruddere's film *Everybody's Famous,* which was nominated for Best Foreign Language Film at the 2001 Academy Awards, a man's job disappears when his factory is closed. He is so emotionally distraught about losing everything that he continues to go to work each morning so that he does not have to reveal his situation to his wife.

Similar to the shame felt after getting fired is the feeling of embarrassment that comes from making a bad business decision or investment. Plenty of people are so ashamed of their business mistakes that they cannot bring themselves to confide in their spouses. Or they lash out whenever their spouse asks about money. Robert is a stockbroker who has never invested in real estate; his entire life he has paid rent. Whenever his wife mentions how much she would like to live in a house, he gets snappish: "Maybe if you didn't spend so much on clothes, we could afford real estate!" he shouts. Clearly, his temper betrays deeper feelings.

Evan, who quit his medical practice to start his own business, got caught in a spiral of shame. "Things were really going downhill financially. I was losing about $40,000 a month. And I just didn't want my fiancée to know about it. I really wanted her to think of me as somebody who had his stuff together. So I never really shared anything with her about it. So, anyway, we go out to dinner, and she has this thing about leaving a big tip, and she will say things in front of the waitress. So we go out to this restaurant, and she says to the waitress, 'He's so cheap,' and she turns to me, 'Sweetheart, don't be cheap tonight, okay?' and I just lost it. I threw the money down on the table and stormed out without saying good-bye. She comes running out after me and we get in a cab, and now I'm trying to embarrass her in front of the cab driver by causing a really big scene." Fortunately, Evan realized how damaging his image-control tactics really were. "She was crying, and I kind of woke up and told her what was going on for me with my business and how bad it really was. She had no idea. From then on things were different. It was like we were partners instead of enemies."

Partner Versus Partner

It is not unusual for partners to be ashamed of one another in front of others when those others are considered to "count more." A typical example is the suburban wife at a cocktail party who makes apologies for her husband's boorish behavior. In Edward Albee's darkly comic exploration of upper-middle-class marriage, *Who's Afraid of Virginia Woolf?*, Martha and George continually apologize to their guests for the other's rudeness. Their mutual embarrassment drives the play toward its heated resolution.

When partners violate the law, the embarrassment is necessarily acute. The same is true when a partner's infidelity is made public.

Even the most right-wing Republicans surely felt sorry for Hillary Clinton when her husband's extramarital activities were finally confirmed in the press.

Different class or ethnic backgrounds can spur feelings of shame. In Chitra Banerjee Divakaruni's story, "Mrs. Dutta Writes a Letter," a young woman is ashamed of her husband's mother's habit of hanging laundry on a clothesline in the backyard. (She is so ashamed she puts her foot down and forbids her mother-in-law from doing it.) In Ben Stiller's film *Meet the Parents,* the primary conceit is that Pam is *not* embarrassed by her boyfriend, Greg, whose last name is Focker and who works as a male nurse, so she blithely brings him home to meet her parents. The makers of the movie and we the audience know that, in real life, a beautiful, well-educated, upper-middle-class woman like Pam would be reluctant to associate herself with a man of such questionable characteristics, unless it was out of daughterly rebellion.

Usually, when partners are embarrassed by each other, they are really embarrassed by their own (self-perceived) flaws. In Divakaruni's story, the young woman is ashamed of her husband's mother, because she is ashamed of her own ethnicity. Our partners are extensions of ourselves but ones we cannot control. So when our partners threaten to make public those aspects of ourselves we wish to keep hidden, we must find a way to stop or change them. In fact, if we can turn our partner into our ideal, then we can seduce ourselves into thinking we have "arrived." My stepmother, who used to be so embarrassed by her own Jewish background that she had her license plates changed when the ones issued to her contained the three letters JAP, would forever correct my father on his "manners." She did her best to make sure that he never acted "ethnic" in public, insisting, for instance, that he never gesture with his hands while speaking.

Embarrassment by association is probably a more common phenomenon than most people realize. It's hard to go from being a single, autonomous individual to one half of a couple, suddenly responsible for all the flaws and failings of another. As human beings we crave connection, yet the relationships we form with one another often make us vulnerable to embarrassment. Sometimes we end up embarrassed by our own perceived flaws, sometimes by the perceived flaws of our partners. Rare perhaps is the relationship untainted by some element of shame.

To the extent that we don't recognize our fears of embarrassment by association, we are easily tempted to use image-control strategies that can only damage our relationships in the long run. But the more you and I are able to recognize when embarrassment is determining our behavior, the more success we are destined to have in our relationships. Self-awareness makes it possible to eliminate the spirals of shame driven by our feelings about sex, money, and social status. To the extent that we *do* recognize and acknowledge our shame-based behavior, we can interact with our partners in a way that allows for mutual self-expression and understanding.

Reconstructing Our Intimate Relationships

As in any area of life, the key to being courageous in our intimate relationships is threefold: (1) dismantling our old beliefs, (2) getting the facts, and (3) taking intelligent risks.

We've already discussed at length the skills of deconstructing old beliefs and getting the facts. The problem is, the longer we've been in a relationship with someone, the more resistant we usually are to questioning our own opinions about the other person (and about ourselves), the more certain we are that we already have all the necessary facts, and the more anxious we usually get about trying new ways of interacting. Self En-Couragement can be especially challenging, because our partners may see our new ways of interacting as a threat. And, in fact, they are a threat, not to our partners but to our established spirals of shame.

Still, deconstructing our old beliefs is essential to transforming our spirals of shame into spirals of intimacy and fulfillment. We get so trapped in our beliefs about sex, money, love, career, housework, and so on, that we become incapable of talking and listening to each other without the protection of our image-control schemes. Our beliefs about what's true keep us alternating between withdrawal, deception, and intimidation. Only when we let go of our beliefs can we be free to act, react, and interact in a more dignified and mature manner.

Any time you find yourself scheming (pulling in, making up a story, or lashing out), the first thing to do is to ask yourself What am I assuming is true that may not be? What am I assuming is true about sex or money or love or family? What am I assuming is true about the way things "should" be?

When you've begun to deconstruct your assumptions, you can focus on the facts. Train yourself to think like a newspaper reporter. Get the who, what, where, and when (forget about the why). Give yourself time to come to a conclusion at a later date. For now, concentrate on what's so. Granted, to get all the facts, you will have to act like a newspaper reporter too. You probably will have to ask a lot of questions. And do a lot of fact checking. Reporters always try to get several sources to confirm a report. I would suggest that whenever possible you do the same.

After deconstructing your beliefs and going on the hunt for facts, you will already be on the way out of your spiral of shame. The next step is to take courageous action to turn that spiral of shame into a spiral of confidence.

Courageous listening is one of the most effective ways to transform a relationship. Courageous listening means listening without giving in to embarrassment or shame. Often, when our partners express criticism or disappointment, we react defensively: We withdraw, we lie, or we lash out. Courageous listening means eschewing those responses. It's the art of taking criticism gracefully. Anyone who wants to become a master in the field of human relationships has to be eager to hear the comments and opinions of others, no matter how critical those comments and opinions may be. Courageous listening takes courage because (childhood rhymes to the contrary) we often think that words can hurt us. They can't, of course, but courageous listening requires bravery in the face of anxiety.

Taking responsibility for what you've done (and forgiving yourself for it) is another key to transforming a marriage or partnership. Much of the time, we're so embarrassed by the mistakes we've made that we take no responsibility for them. We shift the blame to our partners, our parents, our bosses, our coworkers, our neighbors, and so on. But taking responsibility for one's mistakes is a critical step in reconstructing a relationship. Taking responsibility for the past brings a halt to our spirals of shame. When we take ownership of our actions, we are no longer subject to feelings of guilt, embarrassment or self-blame. Taking responsibility doesn't mean feeling *more* guilty or *more* ashamed, or *more* embarrassed. It means acknowledging your role in whatever occurred and letting go of the desire to dump responsibility onto others.

When you have taken responsibility for the past, you are then able to forgive yourself for it. That allows you (and your significant other) to move on. You will also get stronger at forgiving your significant other for the mistakes he or she makes. Then you will be on the path to a truly harmonious relationship.

* * *

Questions to Ask Yourself

What bedroom issues are you being shy about?

When do you become embarrassed/ashamed about money?

What embarrasses you about your partner? Why might your partner be embarrassed by you?

What are you "sure" about in your relationship that might be up for debate?

What would your relationship be like if it were unhampered by any spirals of shame?

* * *

WHAT TO DO WHEN IT SEEMS TOO LATE TO DO ANYTHING

Jared is a rabbi in his thirties. When he was just starting out, Jared agreed to perform a Saturday night wedding for friends of his parents. On the appointed day, Jared was preoccupied with other matters. He spent the evening with a group of friends. The next morning he woke up in a cold sweat. He'd completely forgotten about the wedding. He was mortified. He called his parents to apologize, then he called the bride and groom. There was nothing he could do to undo the damage. His sense of embarrassment and shame was overwhelming.

When you know you've made a mistake and it's impossible to undo what you've done or take back what you've said, it's a horrible feeling. The following tips are for dealing with that feeling when it strikes. They're not intended to push the embarrassment away. In fact, the more you try to push it away, the stronger it will become. Rather, these recommendations are intended to help soften the effects of embarrassment by helping you embrace the circumstances of your situation. As a general rule of Self En-Couragement, when you embrace your circumstances, whatever they may be, feelings of embarrassment usually go away on their own.

1. REMEMBER THE IMAGINARY SPOTLIGHT EFFECT. Even though you may be *positive* that you've made a fool of yourself, other people may not have noticed your blunder. That's not a reason to try to hide your faux pas, but it is a reason to refrain from imagining the worst. Most people are too preoccupied with what others are thinking about *them* to worry about what they think of *you*. You may think you're in the spotlight when, from everyone else's perspective, you're in the shadows. So, first and foremost, it's important to remember the imaginary spotlight effect and the tendency of all human beings to be self-conscious.

Pscyhologist Albert Ellis says we frequently "awfulize" situations: We assume we've done something terrible that others will resent us or blame us for. Here's a story of how one young woman was mortified after making a perfectly human mistake. She used prayer to overcome her embarrassment.

> I had some checks to put in my bank account, so I stopped at the drive-up window of my bank. I took the canister [for depositing items], and as I was putting in my checks, I realized I had forgotten one, so I drove away from the drive-up window and headed back home. Halfway home I realized that I still had the bank canister laying on the seat of my car—I'd forgotten to put it back in its receptacle at the drive-up window. I didn't know what to do. I could only imagine what the bank teller would think of me if I told the truth? What a space cadet! What a dope! What a loser! So, I weighed my options. I could throw it out the window. Put it in the garbage. Return it and tell them I found it on the street.
>
> I started praying. God led me to go home, get whatever it was I had forgotten to complete my banking transaction, go back to the drive-up window, put my items in the canis-

ter, and return it to the teller. When she acknowledged me, I told her how I had forgotten an item and that I'd driven off with the canister. She said, "Thank you," and we went about our day. I had awfulized the whole thing. All my fears turned out to be unfounded.

Before you work yourself up into a frenzy, keep in mind that other people don't have the time to worry about your mistakes. If someone does happen to have a "hissy fit" about something you've done, pity them. You can bet they rarely handle their own embarrassing moments with any sort of grace.

2. BLUSH. Obviously, I'm being slightly facetious. But only slightly. While you cannot will your face to redden, you can, as philosophers would say, allow your own embarrassment "to be," without trying to make it go away. Some people try to stop themselves from blushing, and that only makes matters worse. If you're embarrassed, allow yourself to show it. Have a good laugh at yourself. Allow people to see the real you. Enjoy the silliness of life, and that will allow other people to enjoy it too. Psychologists Thomas Scheff and Suzanne Retzinger observe: "When shame is acknowledged rather than denied, it is of brief duration—usually less than a minute—and serves as a signal, allowing for the repair of damaged [social] bonds. . . . Denial occurs when one is ashamed of being ashamed. Under these conditions, shame becomes recursive and self-perpetuating. Unacknowledged shame builds a wall between persons and groups. A chain reaction occurs, shame building on shame."[1] And Edward Gross, a professor at the University of Washington who has been studying embarrassment for the

past two decades, notes that ". . . research shows that people who are embarrassed, and simply admit to it and then stalwartly carry on, are tremendously well liked." When we pretend that nothing is wrong, despite feeling like something really *is* wrong, we make other people feel uncomfortable. When we admit to being embarrassed, we reveal our humanity and *that* is attractive.[2]

3. LOOK AT THE WHOLE PICTURE. Russell Friedman, executive director of the Grief Recovery Institute, runs workshops for people dealing with loss. Often, people come to his programs feeling guilty or ashamed about what they did or didn't do. Friedman emphasizes the importance of looking at the whole picture: "You have to look at the whole picture of what happened, not just your own part in it. If you only look at your own part, you'll be finished. You'll feel bad forever. No one is ever solely to blame for anything."

4. MAKE YOURSELF MORE VULNERABLE. The best way out of an embarrassing situation is the same way you got into it: by making yourself vulnerable. One thing some people instinctively do is pose a humorous, self-effacing question: "Do you think I'm a total idiot now?" "Do you just want to pretend you never met me?"

You can also invite the other person to open up, which will take the stress out of the situation: "I feel like a fool. Have you ever done something like this?" Nine times out of ten the other person will volunteer an embarrassing incident of his or her own.

You should also ask what you can do to clean up the situation. Say, for instance, you make a mistake on a report at work, and your boss discovers the mistake—after the report has been sent out to the client. Apologizing profusely to your boss is nice, but it doesn't do much from her point of view. A better response is to apologize once, then ask "What can I do to remedy this?" You might want to propose some remedies of your own: "Would you like me to call the client and personally apologize?" Whatever your boss says, do it and then "check in" with her: "Is there anything else you'd like me to do to resolve this situation?" If your boss says no, you can apologize one more time: "Again, I'm really sorry." But *that's it*. And for your own sake, come up with a way to avoid making the same mistake in the future. If that means doing more work, so be it.

5. Do something for yourself or, even better, for others. Embarrassment makes us want to hide and takes an immediate toll on our self-esteem. When you embarrass yourself, you feel badly about your self-worth. It helps, when feeling embarrassed, to do something that will restore your sense of pride. Cleaning the house is one possibility; paying the bills is another. Going to the gym, organizing your files, sending out overdue thank-you cards—these kinds of activities, while they may not seem "fun," will go a long way toward reducing the stress of embarrassment. Don't, however, do them as self-punishment; do them as self-restoration.

Another way of restoring your self-pride is by doing something for others. Volunteering with a charity, giving someone a spontaneous gift, making a friend a batch of cookies—all of these function like magic when it comes to healing a damaged self-image. In fact, the more you can take your attention off yourself and focus it on someone else, the better you will feel.

6. **FIND THE HUMOR IN THE SITUATION.** Every situation is funny if you can get enough perspective on it. Tell the story of your humiliation to a friend, with the aim of making them laugh. If the story is really embarrassing, write a David Sedaris–style essay. Who knows? Maybe you could get it published and start a new career.

7. **WATCH REALITY TV.** Reality TV shows are all about embarrassment. They specialize in giving viewers the opportunity to witness other people's humiliation. Watching reality TV is a good way to mitigate your own feelings of shame.

Writer and social critic Adam Sternberg makes the case for shows like *Blind Date, Dismissed,* and *Survivor,* whose participants routinely embarrass themselves. Sternberg recognizes that these shows can have a therapeutic effect:

> When you cringe at the guy on *Blind Date* who repeatedly dives in for a goodnight kiss only to be spurned eight consecutive times, what you're feeling is not just pleasure at his discomfort but also an acute form of sympathy, even empathy. You're thinking, "Oh my god I could be that person, I have been that person." The best kind of cringe is the one that comes not because we feel superior to that jackass on TV but because we feel a connection to that jackass on TV. And this connection is at the heart of what makes reality TV so satisfying. It's a complicated emotional reaction, a mix of repugnance and sympathy, and the fact that there's

an actual physical manifestation, a cringe, can make an hour of watching *Survivor* or *Pop Stars* or *The Real World* more emotionally rewarding—and draining—than watching the best sitcoms or dramas. This is what makes reality TV worthwhile and worth defending, because however induced, when we cringe, we connect, and this leaves us better off, not worse.[3]

So, when you're feeling embarrassed, you can always turn on the TV and take comfort in the embarrassment of others. After all, shame loves company.

8. CELEBRATE YOUR COURAGE. It's almost impossible to embarrass yourself without doing something at least somewhat courageous. If you're an hour late for work and your boss points it out to the entire staff, you can still acknowledge yourself for not calling in sick. If you steal $100,000 from your company and then your name shows up in the newspaper underneath your mugshot, you can still acknowledge yourself for having had the guts to break the law. Sure, you would have been better off putting your courage toward positive social change, but it's too late to regret what's been done. Besides, you're not hurting anyone else by patting yourself on the back after the fact. Better to enjoy jail than spend the rest of your life regretting the past.

In the wake of embarrassment, make a list of the top five things you are most proud of yourself for. If you want, you can ask someone else to think of five things you should be proud of yourself for.

9. **STICK TO YOUR GAME PLAN.** An embarrassing situation usually makes us want to scrap our game plan and come up with another, preferably one that won't attract much attention. You go up to a group of people at a cocktail party, you introduce yourself, you start talking, you make a joke, it falls flat, You want to crawl away and find another group to talk to. At a party, that might be okay, but in life there are times when crawling away just isn't the answer. There are times when it's important to stick to your original plan, if for no other reason than to prove to yourself that you can't be stopped by embarrassment.

Thom Bierdz, former star of the popular soap opera *The Young and the Restless* (he played rich playboy Phillip Chancellor), quit daytime television but then watched his career go under. After the death of his brother and his mother, he fell into a depression. He couldn't get any work as an actor. With mounting bills, he took a job as a bartender for a catering company. All went well until he was sent to an event that turned out to be a dress rehearsal for the *Soap Opera Digest* awards. "I thought, 'I gotta leave. I've got to run out of here.' . . . I thought I'd look horrible, like a failure or a loser." Many, if not most people would have slipped away quietly before anyone noticed. But Bierdz stayed. "It was interesting to face that fear, and I had a great night. It was cool. I was actually exhilarated."[4]

Sticking to your original game plan is not only advantageous for you, it's also inspiring to others. When you show others that you can't be stopped by embarrassment, you demonstrate the qualities of a courageous human being. That makes a difference for anyone else who's interested in being brave.

chapter 10 Parenthood: Raising Courageous Kids

If you're like most parents, you want your children to be happy, confident, easygoing. You want them to be generous, polite, and hardworking. And while you may never have realized it, you probably want them to be unembarrassable. You want Zoe to get back on her bike after she falls off. You want Nicky to try out for the basketball team even after getting teased by his friends for not being a good player. You want Hannah to wear her favorite dress even after the boys tell her she looks ugly in it. You want your kids to be resilient and socially courageous. As they get older, you want them to have the courage to resist the temptation to go along with the crowd. You want them to be brave enough to say no to their friends when their friends encourage them to smoke, drink, and use drugs.

Unembarrassability is not an easy quality to pass on to children. In fact, the more we try to instill in them a sense of courage, the more they tend to resist. When we push them to go beyond their comfort zone, they become defiantly shy, ever more frustrated and withdrawn. "I don't want to," says the boy bitterly to his father, who is urging him to join the other kids in play. But it's hard as a parent to be relaxed when a child gets easily embarrassed or won't try something new, especially if the child's behavior is reminiscent of your own. When my daughter was two she wouldn't go anywhere near a playground swing. She loved to run around, to climb on the jungle gym, to go down the slide. But she dreaded getting in a swing. Her own trepidation made me tense; I didn't want her to grow up with the same sense of social awkwardness I'd felt as a kid. And even though she was only two, I foresaw years of taunting and teasing: "Jordan doesn't know to swing! Jordan doesn't know how to swing!"[1]

Psychologists, educators, and child-development specialists are just beginning to understand the critical role shame spirals play in personal and social development. Even today, most young people have no one to talk to about feelings of embarrassment, shame, or humiliation, so kids keep their feelings to themselves. They find ways to avoid difficult situations at the cost of their own sense of competence.

But the future is promising. Teachers are becoming more attuned to the emotional lives of their students. School counselors are beginning to recognize that schools are breeding grounds of shame and embarrassment. Principals and curriculum specialists are finding ways to promote openness and honesty in the classroom. There is a wonderful picture book by Todd Parr entitled *It's Okay to Be Different*.

Parents have a crucial part to play in the movement against shame. They can model courage in their own lives and nurture it in the lives of their children. When a child has the ability to triumph over self-consciousness, he or she grows up confident in the knowledge that anything is possible. For kids, especially, the way to turn a spiral of shame into a spiral of accomplishment is to practice the skills of social courage.

As a parent, the most important rule to keep in mind when raising children is this: *If you want your kids to be courageous, you'd better be courageous too!* Kids can smell hypocrisy a mile away. They know when adults are being hypocritical. They know when their parents are saying one thing but doing another. Consider the words of child-development expert Robert Coles:

> The most pervasive moral teaching we adults do is by example: the witness of our lives, our ways of being with others and speaking to them and getting on with them—all of that is taken in slowly, cumulatively, by our sons and daughters, our students. To be sure, other sources can count a great a deal: formal lectures or explicit talks, reading and more reading and discussion of what has been read, reprimands and reminders with punishment of various kinds, churchgoing or synagogue attendance, the experiences of hearing sermons and being told biblical messages, and the moral lessons and the wisdom of our secular novelists, poets, and playwrights—all of that can count a great deal. But in the long run of a child's life, the unselfconscious moments that are what we think of simply as the unfolding events of the day and the week turn out to be the really powerful and persuasive times morally.[2]

If you want your daughter to have the courage to make new friends, then start making new friends yourself. If you want your son to have the courage to admit when he's done something wrong, start admitting when you have. I tell parents, if you want your kids to be courageous, you'd better start being the most courageous person you know.

The flip side of rule number one is equally true: When you're actively developing your own skills of social courage, your kids will develop their own. Kids need very few explicit lessons in life. They are much smarter than we give them credit for. All kids want to be courageous; it's a natural, universal aspiration. Demonstrate your own commitment to being brave, and your kids will readily follow suit.

The following suggestions are intended to help you model the skills of social courage. Use them to break through your own limitations. The sooner you demonstrate bravery, the sooner your kids will too.

1. *When you make a mistake, say so.* Social courage begins with the ability to tell the truth. You can only teach your children to be courageous by modeling honesty yourself. When you make a mistake, say so. Own up to your blunders. You don't have to express a lot of guilt or shame, or get overly dramatic. Just acknowledge mistakes as you make them: "Oops, I forgot to bring the shopping list." "Uh-oh, I forgot to buy a birthday card for Mommy." The more you let your kids know that you are fallible and brave enough to admit it, the more they will be able to admit their own failures with equal grace and dignity.

2. *Share your rejections and disappointments, without any drama.* Your kids want to know when you've had a bad day, so tell them. But stick to the facts. Leave out your opinions. "Why did you have a bad day, Daddy?" "Because I asked my boss for a raise and he said no." "Why Daddy?" "I don't know, sweetheart. Sometimes, you ask for things and people say yes, and sometimes people say no." The less wallowing in self-pity the better. Show your kids that you have perspective on life, but avoid getting philosophical. Kids don't want to hear life lessons; they just want to see how you handle situations that are difficult.

3. *When you're proud of finding a solution to a problem, share that too.* If you impress yourself by finding a solution to a problem, share your accomplishment with your kids: "I needed to call my boss when I was

on the bus today because we were stuck in traffic and I knew we were going to be late. But then I realized I'd forgotten to bring my cell phone with me. I thought, 'What am I going to do?' But then I asked a man on the bus to let me borrow his phone and he did. You've got a smart dad, huh?" As you demonstrate that it is okay to take risks in life, your kids will take more risks too. And as you share your sense of pride, they will discover their own sense of pride as well.

4. *Whenever you hear music, dance.* Kids love to express themselves by running, singing, dancing, kissing, hugging, crying, screaming, and so on. But, for the most part, adults repress themselves in order to seem "mature." Kids learn from watching adults. So if your kids see you repressing yourself, they will repress themselves too.

If you're in the supermarket and you hear music playing over the loudspeakers, dance a little as you go down the aisles. Do some disco. Twirl a couple of times. If other people look at you strangely, take that as a sign you're headed in the right direction. When you feel like singing, sing. When you feel like jumping on a pile of leaves, jump. The freer you are, the freer your kids will be.

5. *Don't pretend to have all the answers.* Kids want to know why things are the way they are, especially when things go wrong. As parents, we're often tempted to give answers that *sound* good: "I'm sure Johnny didn't mean what he said." Or "Your teacher just wants you to learn." These kinds of answers undermine kids' ability to solve problems on their own.

If you don't know what else to say, stick to the word *sometimes*: "Sometimes people are mean. What do you think you should do about it?" "Sometimes teachers get upset. What do you think we should do now?"

The benefits of the word *sometimes* are well illustrated in a story told by Beverly Daniel Tatum, an African-American professor of psychology at Mount Holyoke College, recounting an experience with her son, David. One day when Tatum was picking up David at school, he saw a white mother putting boots on her dark-skinned, biracial daughter. "Why don't they match, Mommy?" he asked loudly, "You and I match. They don't match. Mommies and kids are supposed to match." Tatum was immediately embarrassed, but she managed to remain calm. "David," she said simply, "sometimes parents and kids match, and sometimes they don't."[3]

6. *Have the courage to ask your kids if they feel loved.* Children will have the courage to jump high in life only if they feel confident they have a strong trampoline beneath them to catch them when they fall. Parental love provides that trampoline. Obviously, you love your kids. But do they feel like you do? Or do they feel like you criticize them too much? Or are too busy to care?

Parents who show disinterest, disapproval, or rejection tend to raise children who crave approval from others but never feel satisfied in life.[4] That doesn't mean you shouldn't criticize your kids or that you should treat them like fragile china cups. But it does mean that all criticism should be given in a context of love and support. Find out from your kids if they feel loved and supported before you give negative feedback.

And what if they say they don't? The inclination is to get defensive and protest: "But I do love you! I love you so much!" That won't work. In fact, it's irritating because it's just a way of dealing with your own embarrassment at being told you're a bad parent. Instead, just listen to what they have to say. Really listen. Don't change your behavior. Just keep listening. The more you listen, the more loved they will feel.

7. *Be honest about your own embarrassment.* When you're trying to be the best parent on the planet, it's easy to get embarrassed by your own inadequacies. Joey wants the fifty-dollar toy that Carl has, only you're embarrassed because you can't afford to get it for him. Instead of getting defensive ("You have dozens of toys you never play with") or trying

to change the subject ("Hey, let's get an ice cream"), be open about what you're feeling: "I wish I could get you that toy, but we can't afford it. I'm a little embarrassed about it. Any suggestions?"

Divorce is an issue that often embarrasses parents. Your daughter tells her teacher that she likes her father's girlfriend better than you. When you hear that, you're mortified. But instead of trying to stop her from expressing why she likes Daddy's girlfriend, get interested in her views. Listen keenly without getting defensive. Your kids have a lot to say about life; the more you listen to them, the more you will learn about yourself in the process.

If you're embarrassed by the way your son or daughter dresses, talks, or behaves, say so. But remember to deconstruct your own assumptions before you lash out. Most parents get embarrassed but conceal their embarrassment with self-righteous anger. Better to be open about your own embarrassment, so that you can at least have an honest conversation about the problem.

8. *With boys, demonstrate the courage it takes to show weakness.* Boys grow up thinking it is dangerous to be weak. So they will do everything they can to hide their weaknesses (i.e., their vulnerabilities, their insecurities, their fears). In the long run, this will only make them unhappy, especially when they try to have relationships with women. Parents, especially fathers, have an opportunity to show young boys that it is okay to be vulnerable. By being open about your own insecurities and fears, you can show your son that is safe to be himself.

9. *With girls, demonstrate the courage it takes to stand up for what you believe in.* Girl culture emphasizes friendship over viewpoint. Girls learn at an early age that it is more important to be liked than it is to be strong. In fact, girls often learn that being strong is a fast way to having few friends.

You can do wonders for your daughter by showing her that you are willing to stand up for what you believe in, even at the cost of social opinion. Your daughter may be embarrassed by your determination in the short run, but in the long run she will have a role model for taking a stand and following though on a commitment.

10. *Teach your kids how to accept compliments.* This is a piece of advice I found in Philip Zimbardo's book *Shyness: What It Is, What to Do About It,* and I think it is an invaluable pearl of wisdom. Most kids find it hard to accept a compliment. They're afraid of seeming rude. The problem is, their awkwardness usually comes across as rudeness. They know that, but it only makes the problem worse. So they become shyer and less outgoing.

You can en-courage your kids by gently instructing them in the art of accepting compliments. The best way to accept a compliment, of course, is to smile and say "Thank you." But sometimes it helps to add an extra touch by passing the compliment on to someone else: "Thank you. I just do what my mother tells me." Or "Thank you. I've been blessed with great teachers."

Kids who know how to accept compliments end up feeling more secure in themselves and more willing to strive for high goals. They never have to fear that if they succeed in their goals, they won't know what to say.

PART III

Conclusion

The Craft of Living Courageously

Every time I run into Ellen, she seems "to-gether." She not only looks just right (a slim figure, tailored suits, some but never too much makeup, an expensive haircut), she also has a well-paying job on Wall Street and an aura of self-confidence. But privately Ellen acknowledges that she often feels sad and alone. She is constantly worried about what others think of her, especially since, when she was young, her older sisters teased her mercilessly for being ugly and now, as an adult, most of her friends are, like her, attractive, successful, and put-together. She often comes home from work or an evening out on the town and, in the privacy of her own home, sits down on the couch and cries.

Unfortunately, as many people learn the hard way, outward success doesn't necessarily lead to inner peace or happiness. In fact, the more successful we are, the more insecure we may feel. It's no coincidence that so many people in Hollywood—who are among the richest, most beautiful, most glamorous, most famous people in our society—end up addicted to alcohol and drugs. As one Hollywood star recalls of his heyday: "I couldn't help feeling there was something inauthentic about the whole thing—if not the situation itself, then at least my position in it. . . . And so in time I began to feel like an imposter. It's almost as if I expected someone, at any moment, to kick in my door and tell me the charade had gone as far as it was going to go."[1] If we strive for success in order to prove our self-worth, we set ourselves up for dissatisfaction and disappointment. No amount of success can ever completely drown out our low-frequency fears of not fitting in or not being good enough.

In no small measure we have reached a cultural crisis point in terms of our relationship to shame, embarrassment, and self-consciousness. There is greater pressure than ever before to be attractive, to be successful, to be well-known and well-liked. At the same time, the bar is constantly being raised. We are bombarded by virtually unattainable ideals of physical attractiveness and personal success. Psychiatrist Franklin Schneier and psychologist Lawrence Welkowitz, two experts on social anxiety, conclude that cultural trends are causing people to feel more and more inadequate and insecure. "These trends," they write, "feed feelings of inadequacy, embarrassment, social alienation and withdrawal."[2]

The extent of the problem is demonstrated by the unbridled growth of the image industries. The image industries—the cosmetics, fashion, physical fitness, and plastic surgery industries—represent one of the fastest-growing sectors of the U.S. economy. While the image industries used to prey almost exclusively on women, they now benefit from the anxieties of both sexes. We have all become consumed with how we look.

Throughout this book we have looked at shame spirals, those self-escalating patterns of behavior that make it impossible to interact effectively or in a way that is satisfying for either person in a relationship. Sometimes our shame spirals are obvious even to ourselves; sometimes they are less so. Sometimes, in fact, we cannot see when we are trapped in a spiral of shame. We think our actions are completely rational, completely logical. Suffering from a kind of social aphasia, we cannot see other options. We convince ourselves that the choices we have made are the only choices we could have made. So we go on making similar choices, using similar reasoning to defend them, only to be disappointed and dissatisfied with the results.

Our shame spirals can be very elusive. Part of this has to do with habit. The more habitual our shame responses, the more difficult it is to recognize them for what they really are: impulsive image-control reactions. Just the other day there was a message from a friend on my voice mail. A few days went by and I hadn't called him back. I took a moment to examine my reasons for not returning his call. I had all sorts of legitimate reasons: He probably wanted to do something over the weekend, and the weekend was now past; I was swamped with work; etc. But when I really thought about it, my reasons for not returning his call emerged: He often asked me if I wanted to meet him at the gym. I was feeling ashamed about not keeping to my workout schedule and also about becoming increasingly overweight. I didn't want to have a conversation about it—or to go to the gym to solve the problem—so I just didn't return his call.

The moment we recognize our shame spirals and the ways they affect our relationships, the actions to take become obvious. It never requires a great deal of thought. In fact, it becomes immediately apparent: I should pick up the phone, or apologize, or make a bold request. When we see how we've been engaging in self-defeating patterns of behavior, we can see how to break free from them. That's the beauty of self-awareness: It leads naturally to effective interaction.

You don't need me or anyone else to tell you what to do in life. But if you want to have satisfaction and success in life, you do need to be on the lookout for your own self-defeating patterns of behavior. You need to be skeptical of your own justifications for why you do what you do, why you speak the way you speak, why you believe what you believe. Only a self-skeptical individual has the capacity to grow, to break free, to achieve the extraordinary.

For the most part, however, we lack self-awareness. Even the rampant spread of psychological thinking has largely failed to awaken us to the ways we interact and misinteract in life. We grossly underestimate the costs of our misinteractional moves. We overlook the price we pay for succumbing to self-consciousness.

Almost every day the bus between New York City and Hoboken, New Jersey, is crowded with commuters. The people on the bus all tend to look alike: young white professionals on their way to or from work. Judging by the scarcity of wedding rings, most of them are single. If these same people encountered one another at a cocktail party, they'd make conversation. They'd probably entertain hopes of finding a romantic partner or making useful business contacts. They all hail from the same social class and possess roughly the same moral values and know they have nothing genuinely to fear from one another. It is highly unlikely that any one on the bus is a murderer disguised as a yuppie. This isn't the New York City subway we're talking about. Hoboken is a tiny little town, only a mile square. But on the commuter bus from Hoboken to Manhattan there is virtual silence, day in and day out. Rarely does anyone strike up a conversation with anyone else.

Whether we realize it or not, you and I are constantly missing—or to be more precise, actively avoiding—opportunities for potentially lucrative interaction. We get stopped by our image-control strategies. They prevent us from meeting new people and broadening our interactional networks. We suffer from a kind of perpetual, low-frequency fear of looking foolish. This low-level, almost imperceptible, anxiety shapes the ways we interact—and don't interact—in public. It is the glue that keeps us stuck in our spirals of shame. It has an effect on us as individuals, causing us to miss opportunities for personal and professional advancement, and it has an effect on society as a whole, impeding economic growth and social progress.

It was my stepfather who taught me the value of breaking free from the spiral of shame, of taking risks and speaking to strangers. He never missed a chance to meet someone new. He would talk to strangers on trains, on planes, at restaurants, at sports games, at the theater. When I was a teenager, it was awful. (A British friend of my stepfather's once described him, with classic English understatement, as "somewhat socially aggressive.") But my stepfather's determined sociability allowed him to go from being a mediocre student and the son of a tie maker to a prize-winning journalist with an extraordinary number of personal and professional contacts. Ultimately, by making requests of all the people he'd met over the years, he was able to found and finance one of the most successful nonprofit organizations in the world, Seeds of Peace, a program that brings Middle Eastern teenagers to the United States each summer for conflict-resolution training. When my stepfather died, his passing was announced on the CNN ticker tape, President Clinton called to offer his condolences, teenagers throughout the Middle East wrote letters to express their sorrow, and a memorial service was held at the United Nations with such speakers as UN Secretary General Kofi Annan, Henry Kissenger, and Queen Noor of Jordan. My stepfather believed that every opportunity to meet someone new was an opportunity not to be missed.

Though I'm not a naturally outgoing person, I eventually learned to embrace my stepfather as a role model. And I'm glad I did. I once interjected myself into the conversation of two professors talking on a subway and wound up six months later getting a teaching job at Princeton University. On another occasion, I initiated a conversation on a Hoboken bus with my seatmate, who turned out to be a theater director. I happen to be a playwright, and by the end of our conversation, he was interested in reading one of my plays. Three years later he produced and directed my play, *Baptizing Adam,* in a sold-out, New York City run.

The more we break free from our shame spirals, the more we conquer our fears of looking foolish, and the sooner we can develop new strategies, new approaches, new ways of communicating and interacting that will enable us to achieve mutual satisfaction and mutual accomplishment.

But it's not easy. It takes Self En-Couragement, which includes the willingness to be self-critical, self-skeptical, self-demanding. It also takes action or, more specifically, courageous *inter*action. It takes interrupting someone or interjecting yourself into a conversation or intervening in a conflict. It's often uncomfortable; it's rarely easy. The responses you get may be disheartening. Just the other day I was on a bus and tried making conversation with my seatmate, who was carrying a bouquet of flowers. I complimented her on the flowers and asked her if they were a gift for someone else or for her. She was hesitant to answer my question and looked at me like I might be crazy. Naturally I doubted myself. Was I being a nuisance? Was I ruining her bus ride? But I believe in the value of sociability, and I trust my judgment. I'm interested in knowing as many people as I can. If other people are interested in keeping to themselves, that's their right, but it's not going to stop me from seeking out opportunities to make new connections.

Effective interaction requires first and foremost interaction. When we withdraw, when we hide, when we avoid contact or communication, it's impossible to produce breakthrough results. Likewise, effective interaction requires honesty and vulnerability. When we lie or lash out, we undermine our own chances of real success in life.

As we transform our personal shame spirals into spirals of achievement and pride, we do a service to others and to the community as a whole.

Embarrassment, shame, and self-consciousness weaken the social fabric. When enough individuals rely on image-control tactics, the entire society is affected. Business relations become strained. Workplaces become sites of distrust and anxiety. Family ties are weakened. Schools become dysfunctional. By contrast, when individuals operate at a high level of openness and communication, society as a whole flourishes. It is one of the most crucial principles of the social sciences: Societies do best when interaction is frequent and open. And, of course, for you and I to interact freely and openly we must triumph over our feelings of self-consciousness and break free from our reliance on outmoded image-control strategies.

In this book, I have largely focused on the value of recognizing your own image-control strategies and how they shape your own spirals of shame. But it is now time to emphasize the value of recognizing the image-control strategies of others. One of the benefits of self-awareness is that it facilitates insight into the behavior of others. The more we understand the motives and actions of ourselves, the better we understand those of others. And the better we understand the motives and actions of others, the more effectively we can handle conflict-laden situations. All too often, we project malice onto others when there is none. We mistake pulling in for arrogance, we confuse panic-inspired dishonesty with intentional deception, we see someone lashing out and take it as evidence of obnoxiousness or insensitivity. In this sense, we fail to regard others as interactors operating in an interactional context. We misinterpret the content of daily life (the sayings and doings of others), because we fail to appreciate the context (self-consciousness.) We end up feeling superior, self-justified, and stymied instead of being compassionate, cooperative, and coeffective.

Recently I attended a benefit reception for a charity as a volunteer. At the reception I ran into a rich patron I happened to know socially. He seemed unfriendly and quickly excused himself from our conversation. My first instinct was to take it personally: He didn't think I was worth talking to because I was "only" a volunteer. "Fine," I thought,

"I'm not interested in talking to a snob." But later I realized that there were dozens of possible explanations for his "unfriendliness." Perhaps he was embarrassed because he'd just spilled food on his tie and didn't want anyone to see. Or perhaps he was embarrassed because he couldn't remember my name. Or perhaps he was ashamed because he'd just lost a lot of money in the stock market and no longer wanted to give money to the charity. Perhaps he felt badly for not having invited me ahead of time to sit at his table. Who knows? But there's a very good chance his "unfriendliness" was really just awkwardness and self-consciousness. I would bet a hundred dollars he was trapped in his own shame spiral. Yet my first impulse was to blame him for being rude!

As we develop our ability to appreciate the context of social interaction, we get better at interpreting the content. In other words, as we train ourselves to understand the dynamics of self-consciousness, we become more and more effective at reading the behavior of others. We also tend to become more generous, more empathetic, more forgiving. Life becomes less a struggle of wills and more a mutual endeavor.

I hope by now it's clear that this isn't just a "self-help" book. Embarrassment, shame, and other forms of self-consciousness are social issues. They have a corrosive effect on our interactional networks, from our micronetworks at the office to those macronetworks that surround and connect us all. We share a vested interest in freeing ourselves and others from the constraints of our shame spirals. We share a common need for the freedom to achieve and excel.

There is no need to wait until tomorrow to begin your journey into the world of confidence. You can catch and transform your shame spirals today. You can start that business you've always wanted to start or have that conversation with your sister you've been wanting to have or organize that protest march you've been thinking about. Or simply say hello to the person next to you on the bus. Whether you take a small step or a large one, you will be leading us all down the road of EnCouragement and success.

resources

Note: I have not participated in all of these programs, so I cannot personally testify to their effectiveness. But based on either my personal conversations with the program directors or my examination of their materials, I am confident that these programs offer valuable training in the skills of Self En-Couragement and in transforming spirals of shame into spirals of success. There are probably dozens, if not hundreds, of other programs I could have mentioned, but these will give you some idea of what's out there.

ENLIGHTENED LEADERSHIP INTERNATIONAL   ELI offers programs especially for managers who want to be leaders. They directly address issues of creating trust, inspiring employees, and creating courageous teams. The ELI website is *www.enleadership.com*.

FOUR FREEDOMS   Four Freedoms is a Canadian-based organization that offers sexual workshops for couples who want to break through their blocks and barriers in the bedroom. Their workshops address all the fears that come up in sexual situations. The toll-free number is 1-800-684-5308.

THE GRIEF RECOVERY INSTITUTE   The Grief Recovery Institute offers personal workshops that deal directly with issues of embarrassment and shame. The loss of a loved one often leads to feelings of shame and guilt. The fear of seeming like "a bad person" can make it very difficult to move on. For more information about these workshops, visit *www.griefrecovery.com*.

LANDMARK EDUCATION   Landmark Education is a global enterprise that offers courses designed to give you access to living life powerfully and living a life you love. The foundation course, The Landmark Forum, is 3½ days and includes exercises that deal directly with fear and courage. The Landmark Forum is offered around the world, from New York to Hong Kong, L.A. to Tel Aviv. To register for the Landmark Forum, visit *www. Landmarkeducation.com.*

RADICAL HONESTY WORKSHOPS   *Radical Honesty* author Brad Blanton offers three-day and eight-day workshops. In these programs, "you discover how honesty is the cornerstone of personal freedom, creativity and intimacy. You will experience how direct sharing reduces stress, deepens friendships and opens real possibilities in all areas of life." Courses are offered periodically in varying locations. To find out more about these programs, visit *www.radicalhonesty.com.*

THE POSITIVE COACHING ALLIANCE   The mission of the PCA is to eliminate the shaming, ultracompetitive aspects of youth sports. The PCA offers on-line training programs for parents, coaches, and teachers. *www.positivecoach.org*

STARGATE TRANSFORMATIONAL WORKSHOP   These workshops enable you to identify the physical effects of stored-up fear on your body and to release the fear so that you are freed up and more fully alive. *www.at-easewellness.com.*

URBAN OASIS   Urban Oasis offers workshops in upstate New York on several different topics, all of which address issues of fear and courage. In the "Absolute Living" workshop, "individuals learn how to release attachment to fears and obsessions to be fully present in their own lives." In "Perfect Partnership" participants "are helped to understand that having the courage to listen to their partner and to also express themselves from their heart immediately deepens a relationship and allows for a greater sense of appreciation for each other." *www.yoururbanoasis.com.*

There are now numerous transformational consulting companies that work with organizations to transform workplace relationships (and increase profits). Among these companies are: Daniel Robin and Associates, Gap Intl., JMW Consulting, and High Performance Consulting. Information about these companies can be obtained by visiting their respective websites.

notes

CHAPTER I

1. Traditionally, social scientists have used the clunkier expression "impression management," but I think image control is just as accurate and more vivid.

2. Don Lewittes and William Simmons, "Impression Management of Sexually Motivated Behavior," *Journal of Social Psychology* 96 (1975): 39–45.

3. See, for instance, Mark Muraven, Dianne Tice, & Roy F. Baumeister, "Self-control as a limited resource: Regulatory depletion patterns." *Journal of Personality and Social Psychology* 74 (1998): 774–89; Roy F. Baumeister, Ellen Bratslavsky, Mark Muraven, & Dianne M. Tice, "Ego depletion: Is the Self a Limited Resource?" *Journal of Personality and Social Psychology* 74 (1998): 1252–65.

4. Frans deWaal, "Chimpanzee Politics" in *Machiavellian Intelligence: Social Expertise and the Evolution of Intellect in Monkeys, Apes and Humans* ed. by Richard Byrne and Anthony Whiten (NY: Oxford, 1988), 122–31; see also Charles Ford, *Lies, Lies, Lies: The Psychology of Deceit* (Washington, DC: American Psychiatric Press, 1996), 51.

5. Thomas Gilovitch and Kenneth Savitsky, "The Spotlight Effect and the Illusion of Transparency: Egocentric Assessments of How We Are Seen By Others," *Current Directions in Psychological Science* 8 (1999), 165–69. See also Christina Pozo, Charles S. Carver, A. Rodney Wellens,

Michael F. Scheier, "Social Anxiety and Social Perception: Construing Others' Reactions to the Self," *Personality and Social Psychology Bulletin* 17: 355–62.

6. J. M. Richards and J. J. Gross, "Composure at any cost? The cognitive consequences of emotion suppression," *Personality and Social Psychology Bulletin* 25 (1999): 1033–44.

7. *British Journal of Health Psychology* 6 (Feb. 2001): 1–24; Louis Schmidt, "Frontal Brain Electrical Activity in Shyness and Sociability," *Psychological Science* 10 (July 1999); Monique Cuvelier, "Cringe Factor: Your Body Betrays Signs of Embarrassment," *Psychology Today,* March/April 2002, p. 21; Muraven, et al., "Self-control as a Limited Resource."

8. Freud mistakenly attributed all of childhood shame to the Oedipal complex. Obviously, children feel shame for a wide variety of reasons, most of them having more to do with parental disapproval than with sexual anxiety.

9. Francis Broucek, *Shame and the Self* (New York: Guilford Press, 1991).

CHAPTER 2

1. Thomas Scheff and Suzanne Retzinger, *Emotions and Violence: Shame and Rage in Destructive Conflicts* (Lexington, MA: Lexington Books, 1991), pp. 43–53.

2. Studies show that shyness is sometimes a matter of genetics. Blue-eyed children tend to be more shy than brown-eyed children, for instance. But it is safe to say that most of the time shyness is actually a proactive, image-control ploy.

3. *O,* Feb. 2003, p. 194.

4. On Soros's commitment to philosophy, see Michael Kaufman, *Soros: The Life and Times of a Messianic Billionaire* (New York: Knopf, 2002).

5. The coalition organizers were legitimately worried about how the media would exploit a publicly set goal to pronounce failure. This points to the need for journalists to recognize how much time they spend intentionally trying to embarrass public servants. That time could surely be better spent in other ways.

6. For example, if you aim blindly in your career, you may end up at the top

but leave your colleagues feeling walked-over. If they get the chance, they may try their best to pull you back down.

7. F. deWaal, "Chimpanzee Politics"; see also Charles Ford, *Lies, Lies, Lies: The Psychology of Deceit* (Washington, DC: American Psychiatric Press, 1996), p. 4.

8. See Bella M. DePaulo, Jennifer A. Epstein, and Carol S. LeMay, "Responses of the Socially Anxious to the Prospect of Interpersonal Evaluation," *Journal of Personality* 58 (1990): 623–40; Warren H. Jones and M. D. Carver, "Shyness, Social Behavior and Relationships," in *Shyness: Perspectives on Research and Treatment,* eds. Warren H. Jones, Jonathan M. Cheek and Stephen R. Briggs (New York: Plenum, 1986): 227–38; C. A. Langston and N. Cantor, "Anxiety and Social Constraint: When Making Friends is Hard," *Journal of Personality and Social Psychology* 56 (1989): 649–61.

9. Peter Johnson, "Couric Colonoscopy Prompted Many to Seek Test, Study Says," *USA Today,* 6 May 2002.

CHAPTER 3

1. "The Scofflaw," aired 26 Jan 1995, NBC.

2. Peter Doskoch, "The real truth about lying," *Psychology Today,* Sept./Oct. 1996, p. 16.

3. James Patterson and Peter Kim, *The Day America Told the Truth* (New York: Prentice-Hall, 1991); see also Ford, *Lies, Lies, Lies,* p. 51.

4. William Healy and Mary T. Healy, *Pathological Lying, Accusation and Swindling* (Boston: Little Brown, 1915). The story is repeated in Charles Ford, *Lies! Lies! Lies!,* p. 83.

5. Michael Schaller, *Reckoning with Reagan: America and Its President in the 1980's* (New York: Oxford, 1992); see also Charles V. Ford, *Lies! Lies! Lies!,* pp. 2–3.

6. Kati Morrison, Airdrie Thompson-Gumpy, and Patricia Bell, *Stepmothers: Exploring the Myth* (Ottawa, Canada: Canadian Council on Social Development, 1986); Jeanne E. Moorman, D. J. Hernandez, "Married Couple Families with Step, Adopted and Biological Children," *Demography* 26 (1989): 267–77. A more effective strategy is for stepmothers to prac-

tice what one theorist calls "confrontation and breaking through." This strategy begins with acknowledging one's stepmother status and then working to promote one's own unique qualities as a stepparent. See Marie Dainton, "The Myths and Misconceptions of the Stepmother Identity: Descriptions and Prescriptions for Identity Management," *Family Relations* 42 (1993): 93–98

7. Solomon Asch, "Effects of Group Pressure Upon the Modification and Distortion of Judgments," in *Groups, Leadership, and Men,* ed. H. Guetzkow (New York: Russell & Russell, 1963), pp. 177–90. Did these participants come to doubt their own powers of observation? Or did they merely lie to avoid conflict? In fact, it doesn't really matter. What Asch's experiments show is that many people cannot bear to be different and that they will—consciously or unconsciously—fudge the truth in order to fit in.

8. Dennis Wholey, *The Courage to Change: Hope and Help for Alcoholics and their Families* (Boston: Houghton Mifflin, 1984), p. 219.

9. Carl Rogers, *A Way of Being* (Boston: Houghton Mifflin, 1980), pp. 17–18.

10. Dacher Keltner and Cameron Anderson, "Saving Face for Darwin: The Functions and Uses of Embarrassment," *Current Directions in Psychological Science,* 9 (Dec. 2000): 187–92. See Dacher Keltner and B. N. Buswell, "Embarrassment: Its Distinct Form and Appeasement Functions," *Psychological Bulletin* 122 (1997): 250–77.

11. Mark R. Leary and W. D. Cutlip, "Anatomic and Physiological Bases of Social Blushing: Speculations from Neurology and Psychology," *Behavioral Neurology* 6 (1993): 181–85; Ross W. Buck and J. C. Strom, "Staring and Participants' Sex: Physiological and Subjective Reactions," *Personality and Social Psychology Bulletin* 5 (1979): 114–17.

CHAPTER 4

1. Melvin Lansky, "Violence, Shame and the Family," *International Journal of Family Psychiatry* 5 (1984): 21–40.

2. Bert Brown, "The Effects of Need to Maintain Face on Interpersonal Bargaining," *Journal of Experimental Social Psychology* 4 (1968): 107–22.

See also Lee A. Borah, "The Effects of Threat in Bargaining: Critical and Experimental Analysis," *Journal of Abnormal and Social Psychology* 66 (1963): 37–44; Morton Deutsch, "The Face of Bargaining," *Operations Research* 9 (1961): 886–97; Morton Deutsch and Robert Krauss, "The Effects of Threat on Interpersonal Bargaining," *Journal of Conflict Resolution* 6 (1962): 52–76.

3. Psychologist Willard Gaylin, author of *The Rage Within,* also sees a direct connection between anger and embarrassment. Writes Gaylin: "All the psychological conditions that confront us with a sense of danger are compounded when the emotions we are experiencing are made public. Humiliation is the ultimate degradation. When the 'fact' that we are less than lovable is exposed to the public eye, that we are less than potent is announced in the public space, that we are deprived and inadequate becomes part of the public knowledge, we experience humiliation of the most painful order." This humiliation spawns rage that is often uncontrollable and directed at the nearest, most vulnerable target. See Gaylin, *The Rage Within: Anger in Modern Life* (New York: Simon & Schuster, 1984).

4. Kim Pettigrew Brackett, "Facework Strategies Among Romance Fiction Readers," *Social Science Journal* 37 (2000): 347–51.

5. Helen Lewis, *Shame and Guilt in Neurosis* (New York: International Universities Press, 1971).

6. Jonathan Franzen, *The Corrections* (New York: Picador, 2002), p. 60.

7. *Corrections,* p. 61.

CHAPTER 5

1. Unfortunately, people who are very good at "reading between the lines" in a conversation and interpreting social situations also tend to be among the most aware of the opinions of others and thus the most fearful of embarrassment. Sometimes, ignorance really is bliss. Rowland S. Miller, "On the Nature of Embarrassability: Shyness, Social Skill and Social-Evaluation," *Journal of Personality* 63 (June 1995): 315–40.

2. Michael J. Fox, *Lucky Man: A Memoir* (New York: Hyperion, 2002), pp. 76–79.

3. See Eva Fogelman, *Conscience and Courage: Rescuers of Jews During the Holocaust* (New York: Anchor, 1994); and Ervin Staub, "Helping a Distressed Person: Social, Personality and Stimulus Determinants," in *Advances in Experimental Social Psychology, Vol. 7*, L. Berkowitz, ed. (New York: Academic Press, 1974).

4. Deborah Finfgeld, "Courage as a Process of Pushing Beyond Struggle," *Qualitative Health Research* 9 (Nov. 1999): 803–15.

5. Maureen Neihart, "Systematic Risk-Taking," *Roeper Review* 21 (May/June 1999): 289–91. See also M. Adderholdt-Elliot, *Perfectionism: What's Bad About Being Too Good?* (Minneapolis, MN: Free Spirit Publishing, 1987); Mihaly Csikszentmihalyi, *Flow: The Psychology of Optimal Experience* (New York: HarperCollins, 1990); Joseph Ilardo, *Risk-Taking for Personal Growth* (Oakland, CA: Harbinger, 1992); David Viscott, *Risking* (New York: Pocket, 1977); Betty A. Walker and Marilyn Mehr, *The Courage to Achieve: Why America's Brightest Women Struggle to Fulfill Their Promise* (New York: Simon & Schuster, 1992).

6. Deborah L. Finfgeld, "Courage in Young Adults with Long Term Health Concerns," in *Coping With Chronic Illness: Overcoming Powerlessness*, ed. Judith E. Miller (Philadelphia: F. A. Davis, 2000), pp. 145–64.

7. Myron P. Glazer and Penina M. Glazer, *The Whistleblowers: Exposing Corruption in Government and Industry* (New York: Basic, 1989).

8. Walker and Mehr, *The Courage to Achieve*.

9. The tragedy is that as little John Gottimer Jr. grew up, he eventually got trapped in a spiral of shame of his own. By his twenties, he was avoiding having to speak in public at a cost to his own professional advancement.

10. But when all is said and done, open communication is better than self-censorship. I would rather hear someone say what's really on his or her mind than pretend to be nice while stifling nasty thoughts. Those nasty thoughts will find a way out somehow. Better they be expressed in word than in deed.

11. Matilda Raffa Cuomo, ed., *The Person Who Changed My Life: Seventy-Five Prominent Americans Recount Their Mentors* (New York: Carol, 1999), p. 171.

12. Alex Witchel, "How a D (for Dyslexia) Pupil Rose to Realty's A-List," *New York Times*, Fashion & Style, 2 Feb. 2003.

13. Ellen Langer, A. Blank, and B. Chanowitz, "The Mindlessness of Ostensibly Thoughtful Action," *Journal of Personality and Social Psychology* 36 (1978): 635–42.

14. I am indebted to Bram Towbin for suggesting that I look into Arthur and his legacy.

15. Norman Augustine, "Managing the Crisis You Tried to Prevent," *Harvard Business Review on Crisis Management* (Cambridge, MA: Harvard Business School Press, 2000), p. 22.

16. While most of us focus on hiding our guilt, some people make a show of theirs. They readily use "I'm sorry" to get out of awkward situations. This is called *ersatz contrition*. A good sign of ersatz contrition is constant apologizing. Anyone who has a habit of saying "I'm so sorry" is probably not sorry at all. In fact, ersatz contrition can hide hatefulness or resentment. The resentment may get manifested in genuine mistakes that require apologies, but the constant apologizing that is a result is a sign of a deeper, passive-aggressive dynamic.

17. See, for example, Kazuo Sakai, *The Art of Lying,* trans. Sara Ayona (New York: Red Brick Press), 1998.

CHAPTER 6

1. I love the following scene in Ayn Rand's *The Fountainhead*: "When Keating was called upon to speak, he rose confidently. He could not show that he was terrified. He had nothing to say about architecture. But he spoke, his head high, as an equal among equals, just subtly diffident, so that no great name present could take offense. He remembered saying: 'Architecture is a great art . . . with our eyes to the future and the reverence of the past in our hearts . . . of all the crafts, the most important one sociologically . . . and, as the man who is an inspiration to us all has said today, the three eternal entities are: Truth, Love, and Beauty . . .' "

2. Robert Edelman, *The Psychology of Embarrassment* (New York: Wiley, 1987), p. 142.

3. Edelman, *The Psychology of Embarrassment,* pp. 150–51.

4. In contrast, Francis J. Flynn, a professor at Columbia Business School, says that the asking for—and giving of—help can upgrade an interac-

tional network. Flynn calls the giving of help an exchange. He says that more exchanges mean a more harmonious workplace. As he puts it, "For peer employees, the benefits of increased exchange frequency may include an enhanced affinity for one another and greater understanding of one another's underlying interests and values, which, in turn, lead to a more pleasant and efficient pattern of exchange."

5. Matilda Raffa Cuomo, ed., *The Person Who Changed My Life: Seventy-Five Prominent Americans Recount Their Mentors* (New York: Carol, 1999), pp. 65–66.

6. Jack J. Phillips, Steven D. Jones, Michael M. Beyerlein, eds. *In Action: Developing High-Performance Work Teams,* Vol. 2 (Denton, Texas: American Society for Training & Development, Alexandria, VA, Center for the Study of Work Teams, University of North Texas, 1998).

En-Couraging Yourself

1. Walter Lippman, *Public Opinion* (New York: Macmillan, 1965), p. 10.

2. Mark Leary and Robin Kowalski, *Social Anxiety* (New York: Guilford, 1995), p. 60.

3. Michael Gross, "Jewish Rescue in Holland and France During the Second World War: Moral Cognition and Collective Action," *Social Forces* 73 (1994): 463–96.

4. Wayne Koestenbaum, *The Queen's Throat: Opera, Homosexuality and the Mystery of Desire* (New York: Poseidon, 1993), p. 44.

Chapter 7

1. See also, Tamar Lewin, "Parents' Role Is Narrowing Generation Gap on Campus," *New York Times,* 6 January 2003.

Chapter 8

1. Dennis Wholey, *The Courage to Change: Personal Conversations About Alcoholism* (Boston, MA: Houghton Mifflin, 1984), p. 85.

CHAPTER 9

1. Equally hard to admit, or perhaps even harder, is having sexually abused or assaulted someone else. What could be more humiliating than to admit to having committed such a crime? Yet if people are to move on with their lives (and not stay trapped in a cycle of self-loathing and abuse), they must find a way to communicate openly with someone. For those who are in an intimate relationship, at some point, they will need to confide in their partner.

2. Sitcoms rarely deal with financial conflicts largely because television producers are worried about making shows that hit too close to home. *Roseanne* was a show that boldly defied television taboos against domestic squabbling about money, but its success did not usher in a new era of fiscally concerned sitcom characters or financially centered plotlines. Even dramas tend to stay away from personal finance troubles. Americans prefer escapism to social realism. That's not good or bad; it's just a fact.

3. Interview with Chris Farrel, "Right on the Money."

4. Eugene Raudsepp, "After the Pink Slip: Formulate a Game Plan," *National Business Employment Weekly,* available on-line at *www.careerjournal.com/jobhunting/jobloss/20020813-raudsepp.html.*

WHAT TO DO WHEN IT SEEMS TOO LATE

1. Thomas Scheff and Suzanne Retzinger, *Emotions and Violence: Shame and Rage in Destructive Conflicts* (Lexington, MA: Lexington Books, 1991), pp. 29–20.

2. *http://www.bewell.com/healthy/mind/1999/embarrass/index.asp* (website for HealthGate). Gross wrote *Embarrassment in Everyday Life: What to do about it!* (ETC Publications, 1991).

3. *This American Life,* 13 April 2001, NPR.

4. *IN,* 9 September 2002, p. 15.

CHAPTER 10

1. This behavior continued until one day her perspective changed, and she fell in love with swinging. Now, we can't pass a playground without cries of "Daddy, just one swing, pleeeease?" I don't think I can take any credit for her transformation except to say that, as a father, I have always attempted to model courageous behavior myself.

2. Robert Coles, *The Moral Intelligence of Children* (New York: Random House, 1997), p. 31

3. Tatum, *"Why Are All the Black Kids Sitting Together in the Cafeteria?" And Other Conversations About Race* (New York: Basic, 1997), p. 33. Tatum says that many white parents do not know how to respond when their children make observations about skin color. "Imagine this scenario. A White mother and a preschool child are shopping in the grocery store. They pass a Black woman and child and the White child says loudly, 'Mommy, look at that girl! Why is she so dirty?' (Confusing dark skin with dirt is a common misperception among White preschool children.) The White mother, embarrassed by her child's comment, responds quickly with 'Ssh!'" Tatum says that a better response might be, "Honey, that little girl is not dirty. Her skin is as clean as yours. It's just a different color. Just like we have different hair colors, people have different skin colors." She warns that by failing to give an adequate response (that is, by merely panicking with embarrassment) parents teach children that talking about race is taboo. One day when Tatum's own son came home from school he asked if he were black because he drank "too much chocolate milk." This was how his skin color had been explained to him by one of the other (white) boys in his class. Tatum told him that his complexion had nothing to do with how much milk he drank. She said, "Your skin is brown because you have something in your skin called melanin. Melanin is very important because it helps protect your skin from the sun." She went on to explain that, while the white boys had melanin in their skin too (which was why they got tanned when they went to the beach), he had the most of anyone in his class.

4. J. D. Allaman, C. S. Joyce, and Virginia C. Crandall, "The Antecedents of Social Desirability Response Tendencies of Children and Young Adults," *Child Development* 43 (1972): 1135–60.

CONCLUSION

1. Michael J. Fox, *Lucky Man: A Memoir* (New York: Hyperion, 2002), pp. 110–11.
2. Cited in Franklin Schneier and Lawrence Welkowitz, *The Hidden Face of Shyness: Understanding and Overcoming Social Anxiety* (New York: Avon, 1996), p. 113.

glossary of terms

Awfulizing A term from rational-emotive therapy that refers to the habit of assuming the worst will come of a simple mistake.

Bench warming A type of pulling in that amounts to not competing in a given arena; "dream deferral."

Circumlocution A type of pulling in that involves speaking in vague or otherwise unclear terms

Costrategies Image-control strategies used in tandem by two or more interactors.

Deconstructing your beliefs The practice of turning your skills of skepticism on your own beliefs about what is embarrassing.

Defrosting the facts Telling the truth after having lied.

Disidentifiers Comments made to obscure the truth that are something short of actual lies.

Dissocial situations Situations in which individuals in close proximity fail to interact.

Dyadic encounters Interactions between two individuals.

Embarrassment-anger cycle A common phenomenon in which we lash out, then become embarrassed about having lashed out, so we lash out more, etc.

Emotional concealment A type of pulling in that involves the suppression of the emotions

Extra items Things on which we spend our financial, psychological, or emotional resources as a form of image control.

False promising "Deception in advance"; making promises you know you don't intend to keep.

Goal shy The state of wanting to avoid setting clear, challenging goals.

Going naked Making oneself vulnerable; a form of courageous interaction.

Green thoughts Thoughts that encourage interaction.

Image-control ploys Strategies we use to influence the ways others view us.

Imaginary spotlight effect The tendency to think that others are paying more (and negative) attention to us than they really are.

Interfearance Fear of getting in trouble that interferes with the ability to interact effectively.

Lashing out An offensive response to embarrassment and/or potential embarrassment; an image-control ploy.

Misinteraction An interaction that is inappropriate for a given set of circumstances.

Network A group of people with whom one regularly interacts.

Nonobjection The practice of allowing another person to persist in believing a false assumption. Stepparents, for instance, often fail to object when others assume they are biologically related to their stepchildren.

Paradoxical intention The process of trying to do that which you don't want to do; a concept developed by Viktor Frankl.

Pulling in Withdrawal from social interaction; an image-control ploy.

Red thoughts Thoughts that discourage courageous interaction.

Self En-Couragement A process of training and developing oneself to be courageous in social situations.

Shame spiral The spiral that results after self-consciousness leads to image control, which then leads to a misinteraction and miscommunication, and then further self-consciousness.

Social courage Courage in everyday, social situations; distinct from both physical courage and moral courage.

Stage flight (proactive shyness) A type of pulling in that involves a retreat from communication.

Success spiral The spiral that begins with courageous interaction and results in pride, which leads to more courage and success.

Taking the mike Speaking up even when you don't want to.

Trumping up the truth Deception to avoid embarrassment, an image-control ploy.

Yellow thoughts Thoughts that begin to encourage interaction; yellow thoughts begin with the word *maybe,* as in "Maybe I *should* say hello."

acknowledgments

Numerous people were helpful in the writing of this book, including Lionel Tiger, Harriet Lerner, Thomas Scheff, Carl Semmelroth, Charles Ksir, Carl Hausman, Tony Medley, Steven Soifer, Jodi Wilgoren, Stephanie Capparell, Edmund Morris, Kevin Newbury, Chris Meyers, Ken Heck, Lisa Krause, Vanesssa Avery, Lisa Laplante, Barbara Calvano, Terriane Falcone, Tom Hayes, Ross Cheit, Eric Schneider, Cynthia O'Neal, Bram Towbin, Nan Braman, Mykel Dikus, Melissa Levis, Ari Fritkis, Rob Anderson, Clive Swersky, Pam Coles, Robert Florida, David Wrisley, Susana Nery, Nancy Peltz-Paget, Harry Spence, Deborah Roth, Marci Winograd, Teddi Winograd, Scott Yardley, Tom Wojutnik, Jason Schmidt, Marilyn Miles, John Maturo, Leo Carey, Evan Beyer, my father, Ronald Smith, my mother, Janet Wallach, and my brother Michael Wallach. No one inspired me to be courageous more than my late stepfather, John Wallach.

I am immensely grateful to the extraordinary teachers I've had over the years at Harvard, Brown, and Georgetown Day. A special thanks to Allan Brandt, Donald Fleming, the late Roger Henkle, Clay Roberson, Norrine Mack, Gail Massot, Charles Psychos, Andrea Oram, Laura Rosberg, John Burghardt, Janet Hahn, Susie Ryan, and Kevin Barr.

There is no education in the world like Landmark education. I want to thank all the Seminar Leaders and Landmark Forum Leaders for who they are and what they give to others. Special thanks to Joyce Pike, Gaby Jordan, Joanne Humphreys, and David Cunningham.

I would not have had the opportunity to work with young people if it had not been for the History of Science and History Department Faculties at Harvard, the History Department faculty at Princeton University, the Psychology Department faculty at Marymount Manhattan College, and the staffs of Seeds of Peace, Prep for Prep, The After School Corporation, and the Elie Wiesel Foundation for Humanity. Special thanks to Toby Simon, Lucy Friedman, Bobbie Gotschalk, Tim Wilson, Meredith Katz-Gancher, and Marieke van Woerkom. I am also deeply grateful to Sue Anne Morrow and Georgia Nugent at Princeton and to Peter S. Bearman at the Institute for Social and Economic Research and Policy at Columbia.

Many of my thoughts for this book stemmed from research I did for a piece for the *New York Times Magazine*. Though the piece was never published, the opportunity to do the research and writing was invaluable. My thanks to Ariel Kaminer for that opportunity. I also benefited from the opportunity to write for the *Advocate,* so my thanks to *Advocate* editor Bruce Steele.

Special, special thanks to Admir Imami and Gabriela Tobal for their daily encouragement and support.

I am truly grateful for the work done by my outstanding research assistants: Nicole Fabian, Justin Prunell, Kathleen Van Dyk, Owen Wholley, George Gottimer, and especially Max Melion.

Finally, this book would never have been possible without the unflagging support of my agent, Andrew Stuart, and the vision and effort of my editor, Sara Carder.

index

DAVID ALLYN, PH.D., gives lectures and conducts workshops on Self En-Couragement and transforming Spirals of Shame into Spirals of Success. If you are interested in scheduling a presentation or workshop, contact David Allyn directly at dallyn@optonline.net.

www.spiralsofsuccess.com